BITE BY BITE

ALSO BY
AIMEE NEZHUKUMATATHIL

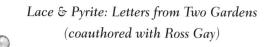

Lace & Pyrite: Letters from Two Gardens
(coauthored with Ross Gay)

World of Wonders: In Praise of Fireflies,
Whale Sharks, and Other Astonishments

Oceanic

Lucky Fish

At the Drive-In Volcano

Miracle Fruit

BITE
BY BITE

Nourishments & Jamborees

AIMEE
NEZHUKUMATATHIL

An Imprint of HarperCollins*Publishers*

HarperCollins books may be purchased for educational, business, or sales promotional use. For information, please email the Special Markets Department at SPsales@harpercollins.com.

Ecco® and HarperCollins® are trademarks of HarperCollins Publishers.

The food writing prompts on page 209 originally appeared in the January/ February 2023 issue of *Poets & Writers Magazine* (pw.org).

FIRST EDITION

Designed by Jennifer Chung
Illustrations © Fumi Nakamura

Library of Congress Cataloging-in-Publication Data has been applied for.

ISBN 978-0-06328226-1

24 25 26 27 28 LBC 5 4 3 2 1

For my family, my beloveds—

CONTENTS

INTRODUCTION

I have a confession to make: I don't really like cake. Oh, I love what happens when a cake is offered up at gatherings—the shiny eyes, the songs, the quick lick-away of frosting from a thumb. And I adore cake-adjacent sweets like tarts, waffles, muffins, trifles, and my favorite—tiramisu. But I realized what I love most about cake is the time and energy spent making something celebratory. To make. In fact, the origin of the word *poet* comes from the Greek word that means "to make." No surprise then, as one who writes poems and has taught others how to write poems for decades, that I turn my "making eye" to food. And don't worry, I actually *love* to make cakes: flour powdering my apron, the pans and bowls piling up, serving them up on a pretty dish—that is nourishment. When I sit and we share stories and opinions and worries and wishes—that is nourishment. That slow time when we sing and savor? Nourishment.

I especially savor the times my family eats meals on our back porch here in Mississippi, a tiny dog underfoot and hoping for a mistake. I'm so grateful to see my elderly parents gather around my own table while I implore them to just sit and relax so that my husband, Dustin, our boys, and I can cook. (My parents, like so many of our parents, do not know how to relax and be served!) And I'm thankful for my friends laughing and smacking the tables so hard while they cackle into the night. I adore having grad students over for a meal around our firepit—another kind of teaching. When I guide international students in making s'mores in our backyard, their first crumbly, decadent bite breaking into a sticky smile—no institution hovering over us—it's so clear we are learning how to make joy for ourselves, for one another.

When my sons, now fourteen and seventeen, had their first bite of solid food (bananas), my heart almost knocked out of my chest. I was ecstatic: bite by massive bite, they smiled so big at this new creamy, scrummy taste. Each day felt like a new adventure to try: Sweet potatoes? *Yes.* Pureed carrots? *More.* Peas? *Okay, hold up, wait a hot minute—let's figure this one out.*

But what of the food that has served me and that I now serve to my beloveds? Where does the food come from? What have people who have come before me done that I might have this spice in my cabinet, this fruit in my fridge? This fish, smoked and dried in my freezer for a special occasion? This honey from my friends' son in Jackson?

This book is a bite of personal and natural history, a serving if you will—scooped up with a dollop of the bounty and largesse of the edible world. It's also an exploration of the banquet of saporific wonder that the planet offers us, the wonder I hope you carry back to share with others.

I wrote this because, as a poet of the natural world, I had questions that begat questions, such as: Where did some of my favorite spices come from? Why do I associate mint with maternal love? Why do pawpaws make me think of promises? These are questions I will pursue for the rest of my days. For what is home if not the first place where you learn what does and does not nourish you? The first place you learn to sit still and slow down when someone offers you a bite to eat?

I write about my family to insist upon our presence in the world, even when, not that long ago, stories like mine have been disregarded or ignored. I know food can be fraught and a source of pain for so many people, but where are the appetizing origin stories of care and sustenance? Perhaps we can kaleidoscope other depictions and try to make it easier for hundreds of thousands of hardworking families to share stories like these (untold, overlooked), so the next generation can find themselves in books or television or movies as they grow up. I want to celebrate with you how my family and friends gather and what we remember, and share my curiosity about where food comes from, how it makes us feel connected to a landscape that hasn't always loved us back.

What we think about food is a portal into our own personal histories, ourselves—and most lovely of all, it's a chance to deepen our connection with others. Noticing food means being aware of the scent and ooze, the sizzle and slip. The peck and the puff. Taking stock of *all* your senses. The crackle crunch of lumpia means knowing it was made by someone who celebrates me and my mother's heritage, and with that carries a hint of replicating her care and attention toward me. It means, too, that I'm likely at a party. The sharp and juicy bite of an apple zips me back to orchards in western New York, selecting apples with my toddlers waddling behind me like ducklings in their bulky little sweaters and rosy cheeks, still dusted with sugar from cider donuts eaten hours before. I believe details like these can ignite a footpath back to your own reflections, your own *nourishments*, and the times people gathered around you in *jamboree*.

In these pages, I hope you can also see I'm not fond of sugarcoating the past—so many foods have a history that is difficult to reconcile and a present that has shed production origins gentler to the planet that it's hard to ignore a most uncertain environmental future. Taking a holistic look into what we consume, we see how we are what we eat. And what we eat can help us grow into our scrumptious selves. Cooking is all about chemical reactions, a transformation from raw to cooked, from ingredient to dish. There is beauty in the transformation, not just the result. Seeds to plant, blossoms to fruit, children to adults. These essays remember merriment. But these essays also remember struggle—sometimes tart and sometimes sweet.

It all comes back to this making, this poem-ing, even if you don't consider yourself a poet: when you move your jaw to chew on food, I can't help but honey-smile—unless you're chewing with your mouth open (in which case please fix yourself and then we can be friends). A honey-smile is a slow smile that starts somewhere inside before it ever bubbles up, becoming effervescent on a face. It means that at least *that* day, *that* hour, *that* minute, you taste the delicious world I offer up—you nourish your body with it. It becomes *our* nourishing because we take care of one another. Your good and glad heart pounding all the while, happy for another day to come to the table. And my heart is glad for that too. And I'm certain other hearts will rejoice, and soon others, even more than we might come to know in our lifetimes. This is a feast, a slowdown.

Come—sit next to me.

BITE BY BITE

RAMBUTAN

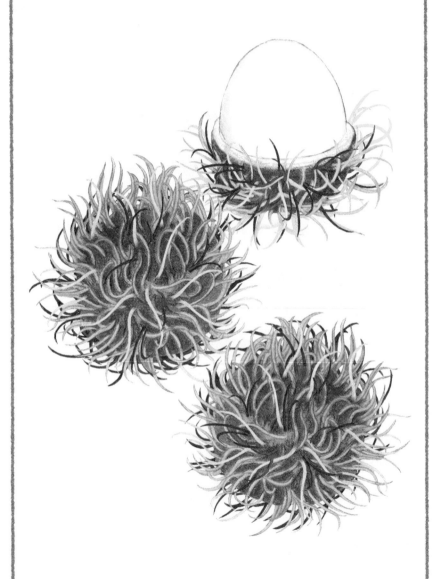

I n six hundred or so years of Nezhukumatathils, not a one had ever attended a middle school dance, so you can imagine how imperative it was that I chose the correct hairdo for the occasion. I am thirteen and toweling off from my shower at home, a mental institution in rural western New York. No, I'm not a patient. My mother is a psychiatrist there, and so for four years— those oh-so-crucial puberty years—we lived at the Doctor's Quarters—a row of three hefty brick houses atop the hill of what was then called the Gowanda Psychiatric Center. I am in a hurry to meet my friends Heather and Sara at the park downtown for ice cream and because of the idea: There Might Be Boys There.

I have my hand on the doorknob when I catch a glimpse of myself in the half fogged-up mirror. Huh? I squeak-squeak rub the mirror in circles for a better view. I remember I audibly gasped. There they were, as if I shampooed them *in* somehow—then *pop!*—curls. What once was just silky waves and bounce for as long as I could remember or care to notice was now bona fide curls. I'm talking *ringlets*.

I swept my hand over the damp curls in disbelief. All I did was comb out the messy tangle and let it air-dry. I thought of all the commercials for hair products that were so common in the mid-eighties: the fluorescent colors of Dep hair gel; L'Oréal, in their jaunty red, yellow, and blue Mondrianesque color-block-designed bottles; and of course, the purple mystique of the Aussie Hair Care line—from Australia (so *exotic*)—where every gel and spritz spray smelled like grape Kool-Aid.

The Malay word for hair is *rambut*, and it's only fitting that the fruit with the wildest curly spinters radiating from its bright scarlet skin—like a tiny red wig fit for the creepiest of clowns—

would be named *rambutan*. In 1912 it was introduced to the Philippines from Indonesia, and soon evergreen trees grew heavy with clusters of twelve to fifteen fruits. Inside the furry-looking red skin, the syrupy smooth flesh—the aril—glows with perhaps the lightest blush, almost translucent, smelling fresh and earthy, like the rocks you find under a running river.

Rambutan trees get to be about fifty to eighty feet tall and produce fruit twice a season. The individual drupe itself is oval, about the length of a double-A battery, and inside is a single glossy, dark seed whose oil can be extracted and used for cooking. When I think of rambutan, I think of the quote from Virginia Woolf: "Blame it or praise it, there is no denying the wild horse in us."

I suppose *the wild horse in me* is best represented by my hair. But I cringe to think of all those years of wanting it to be blond or straighter, only because I was surrounded by that color and texture, and just wanted to fit in. I don't know if I would have believed it, but I *wish* someone had told young Aimee that even though it didn't seem like it in these teeny rural towns, black hair is the most common hair color in the world. Madonna was the biggest pop star on the planet at the time, and when she skyrocketed to fame, her naturally brunette hair was dyed blond (and stayed blond) throughout most of my adolescence, with a quick detour back to brunette during her "Like a Prayer" phase. And I definitely took notice that she sported a wild and messy tumble of curls in arguably the most controversial video of her career, the one that caused so many to turn their backs on her and even boycott Pepsi.

Up until the day my curls appeared, I was forbidden to use any sort of hair product. My Filipina mother, perhaps trying to exert some control over her American-born daughter in a teenage world she didn't understand, always had rules like *No reading magazines close to dinnertime! No phone calls after dinner! No blowing bubblegum bubbles! No makeup! No hair spray!* But now I had curls. I needed to *style* the curls. You couldn't just yank up your curls into a giant ponytail. That would never do. Remember, this was the eighties. Curls were all about being scrunched and crunched in gels, mousse, and styling spray. Some girls from gym class styled their hair in the locker rooms with all three. And no matter what, your bangs *had* to stand taller than your poufiest curl. In short, if you had curls in the eighties, you needed hair product. Period. I changed into clothes as quickly as possible and ran down the stairs to show my hair to my mother, who was cooking breakfast. But it was clear my mother was not going to budge.

"But *why not*, Mommmm?" I kicked at the legs of the wooden dining table while she chopped tomatoes.

"Hair spray dries your hair too much. In two years, you will have no hair. No more use for hair spray! Too young for hair spray!" Chop-chop. Chop. She slid the diced tomatoes into the omelet that was already sizzling on the stove.

She wasn't changing her mind, so I'd leave for school with a small poodling of hair and return in the afternoon to brush out the more than four-inch-high confection of bangs before my mother returned home. I would sneak free sprays in the junior high girls' bathrooms from Heather, she of the cute mini-cans of aerosol Aqua Net in her giant purse.

At one point, I think I had the same amount of hair in the front of my face (which is to say, anything in *front* of my ears) cut into wide, wavy bangs as on the entire back of my head (anything behind my ears). I am twelve. The sketchy lady from Fantastic Sam's hair salon (who smoked while she cut my hair) divided my hair laterally and made the front half all bangs, and the back half—a bizarro she-mullet. This lady teaches me how to use a curling iron. "Yous gotta pouf it, hon. Pouf it!" While she twists and clamps a section of my shelf of slightly damp bangs up off my head a good three inches, she takes a giant can of Aqua Net and sprays the whole thing—iron and all. My hair steams and sizzles into a tiny cloud over my head, and somehow this feels satisfying to me. I watch her very carefully so I can re-create this on Friday nights when I stay home with my family and watch *Miami Vice*.

"Geez, whatcha got your hair done up for," my sister asks, snacking on gummy bears beside me on the couch.

"It's Friday! It's just in case." I cross my arms in front of me and sigh as if she should already have known the answer. But we both know there is no "just in case." There's not even a "Maybe, just maybe." There is only the satisfaction of sitting there, my hair *done*—with a full, dark pouf high atop my head, trying not to show that I am enjoying watching television with my parents after all, instead of being allowed to watch a PG-13 movie downtown with the rest of my friends.

No one asks the rambutan about its messy hair. They just know that if you want a rambutan, you're gonna have to deal with the wild and unruly spinterns. I want to tell you of the years spent blow-drying, ironing, pulling and tugging my hair to straighten it out, but that exhausts me. The hours spent examining my hair in the back with a handheld mirror, wondering what color I should dye it to turn it somehow lighter than this darkest chocolate brown. Anything I could do to it to prevent total strangers from asking me, "What *are* you?" Anything to look more like Sara, Americ, Debby, Stephanie, Jennifer—anyone but me.

I want to tell you of the first time I visited my grandmother in India during monsoon season, and she (fresh from a bath) had joined me on the couch, where I was reading and pouting because I was being eaten alive by mosquitoes. Until then, I had never seen my grandmother wear her hair in anything but a solemn, long braid down her back or wound into a low knot at the base of her head. But when she sat down next to me, I saw her hair in all its glory for the first time *ever*—long, dark, luxurious curls whipped into neat ringlets. My father never told me about this, even when he heard my surprise and subsequent tirade about hair gel the day my hair suddenly turned curly. This tiny woman I saw mainly through pictures that were sent to us in mysterious red, white, and blue envelopes—this woman in flesh and bone and soft brown skin—this woman had the *same* hair as me. Until that moment, I had never seen anyone with the same texture of hair as mine—no model in a magazine, no one from school, even my father, who was almost completely bald, and my mother, who had thick wavy hair to be sure, but no curls, no dark fall of ringlets. Not even my younger sister (who was sometimes mistaken for my twin when we were little) has hair like me. I was speechless. My grandmother must have been uncomfortable with my staring.

"What is wrong? Your mouth is open. Too much mosquito?"

When I didn't answer, "Too much mosquito?" she repeated.

I closed my mouth and shook my head. "Not too many mosquitoes. Your hair—it's, it's . . . beautiful."

My grandmother smiled, the only time I ever saw her embarrassed, and quickly changed the subject. "But you have hair like this too, no? Let's go get some ice cream. Too hot to be inside today." When she walked away to summon the driver, I saw her smiling as she straightened out her turquoise sari.

I want to tell you that there in India is when I made peace with my hair, but that would be too easy. Of course, one could say that as I grew older, my focus turned to other things—a house, a husband, two kids, a geriatric dog, and of course my writing and teaching. But when I see a bowlful of rambutan I'm reminded of the untamed and messy spinterns. I'm reminded of my quiet and delicate grandmother, wrapped in tissue-thin elegant saris but who, in her housedress at night, would take her long hair out of her tight braid and let those ringlets unspool and unspool down her shoulders, a dark waterfall across her back. I'm almost fifty now, and my grandmother does not walk on this earth anymore. I know now that my hair is meant to flap and race the wind and salted air. I unplugged the iron years ago. Let the questions of what is beauty and what is not-beauty fruit down your back. I can't bear anything less than the weight of the same waterfall from my grandmother. No saddle, no harness. It took me decades to do so, but now I embrace the dark wildness of my hair—my rambut, such spring and coil—which refuses to lie down for any iron. Any heat. Most days it's a mess. And that's fine by me. It gallops untamed—not even stopping if you try to offer it a crumbly cube of sugar.

MANGO

I am the daughter of a man from India and a woman from the Philippines. They have argued all my life about whose mangoes are the sweetest, the best. Both have asked me to take sides, and for years I've refused until now. Alphonso mangoes, hands down. From India.

This is a self-portrait. When I was in graduate school, I used the word *mango* in a poem for workshop. This class was run in the traditional workshop mode of "the poet stays quiet after reading her poem aloud while the rest of the class and professor discuss the poem as if she isn't there. She just takes notes silently, with a poker face, whether or not she agrees with what is being said." I knew the poem definitely needed work—I don't think I ever quite figured out syllabics, and I'm sure the title could have used some rewriting—but I never expected what happened next.

After the initial minute or so of awkward silence once I read the poem, there was the pause of no one wanting to be the first to speak. Until someone announced that he thought the word *mango* should be footnoted or italicized so that people know it is a fruit. To explain, to define. And someone else agreed, and as is the case with so many workshops of this nature, another agreed, until the whole thirty minutes was spent discussing exactly how (not if) the word *mango* could be carefully deployed in this poem. Not a single other comment or question or bite of advice was plucked from the stale air that day. I am ashamed to admit it, but I went home and cried. This is a self-portrait.

But then the next week, I doubled down on my use of the word *mango* in my next poem. And the next. And have not stopped, some twenty years later.

The problem with saying the Alphonso mango is the sweetest

mango is then having to defend it all the time, especially if you have a Filipino mother. Named for the Portuguese colonizer of Goa, Afonso de Albuquerque, this mango originates in Brazil, but when planted on the shores of India, the combination of salt air from the Arabian Ocean and the natural acidity of the soil created a new variety.

The name *mango* most likely comes from my dad's language—the Malayalam word *manna*, which the Portuguese adopted as *manga* when they came to Kerala in 1498, during the frenzy of the spice trades. Because mangoes are extrasensitive to the climate and the actual soil where they take root—the terroir—scientists estimate over a thousand varieties in India alone.

And is it enough for my Filipino family and friends to say that while the Alphonso is the sweetest, I have the best memories of the Carabao variety, and to not take my judgment too harshly (or seriously)? *The Guinness Book of World Records* actually lists that Philippine mango as the sweetest in the world. And a couple from Iligan City in Mindanao holds the record for producing the biggest mango in the world, weighing in at about 7.7 pounds, or the weight of a small cat. There are plenty of accolades for Philippine mangoes, so take my Alphonso opinions with a grain of . . . sugar. This is a self-portrait.

Origin of the Mango

Of course my parents can't agree: my father says
       one of its flat stringy seeds floated all the way

from India   and just happened   to land
on the Philippine shoreline.   Anything good

          comes from   India   according to my father:
swirls of calligraphy, counting, the darkest   purest gold

          hammered into rings   and loopy bangles,
paprika, and web-thin silks   that sent hundreds

          of pirates   in a frenzied search   to the East.
          But mangoes
My mother doesn't buy it.   She says The Queen Fruit

          of her beloved islands   came from a tree
growing   in the spot   where a Filipina named Melanga

pierced her heart   through   with a knife. The girl's
          parents   wanted her   to marry someone

          she did not love (a regular Juliet).   The tree grows
bold and   thick in the swell   of winter, pushes

out a dozen heart-shaped fruits   so we won't forget.
          I think of my parents—their hands   slip
          into mangoes

          with knifeblade—fingers fly   lightly   over
          the skins.
          Different countries,   same blood   hungry

for this fruit.   Its flesh   like cold sweetmeat, fibers
spun
          gold, sweet pulp   in the teeth.   The fight

over the seed—who gets to suck   each sugary fiber
          from the pit—only curls their wet hands   together

even more.   Only gets more gold juice, the right story.

Mango season in India lasts from May through June, about
sixty days or so. Spanish explorers brought mangoes to Mexico in
the 1600s, and the first recorded attempt to introduce the mango

into the United States came in 1833 in Florida. The tradition of marrying two mango trees as a signal of trust sometimes still occurs in India: among farmers who want to seal their friendship, it is common for ceremonies to be organized in which two trees, one from each farmer, are joined together in a "marriage." And what a sweet symbol of everlasting friendship—mango trees can live for hundreds of years, and they continue to bear fruits even after two to three hundred years.

After my first year in graduate school, where my white classmates tried to decree what words were too foreign for their ears, my younger sister and I traveled to India by ourselves to spend time with our sweet grandmother. Every time we sat down at her table, we had strips of mangoes sliced up for us, orange-yellow, the brightest color of the meal. If you happened to do a quick scan of the room, you'd have thought golden orioles perched at each place setting. When our grandmother arranged to have saris custom cut and made for us, while we oohed and aahed over the beautiful bolts of fabric, each boutique offered us chilled green boxes of Frooti on a stainless-steel tray, the popular mango juice advertised on billboards and on TV commercials. This is a self-portrait. Hard to ever be testy from the heat when you have aunties offering you Frooti. *Frooti? More Frooti? Are you hot? You need Frooti!*

When I was pregnant with my first son, I used to joke he was a quarter Indian food, a quarter Filipino food, a quarter pineapple, and a quarter mango. That later estimation was because when I was four months pregnant with him, I first felt him kick and flutter inside me any time I ate a mango. My husband and I made the trip to my mother's small village in northern Luzon before a week in Manila with relatives. We wanted to be in the province for New Year's Eve celebrations, even if that meant braving the isolated roads for a five-hour drive after a sixteen-hour plane ride. Day or night, after a few chilled slices, I'd feel the starry flash and sparkle in my belly— like a small fish caught in a tidepool. This is a self-portrait.

 ˙ It was there that Dustin learned the exquisite joy of snagging the prized mango seed first, eating and sucking the juice right off the tiny fibers, the sweetest part of the gold flesh. He would slice the thick cheeks of the mango away from the long, flat pit and slide-slurp the sweet flesh directly from the skin. I was always ambivalent over how to eat one if it wasn't diced up for me already, and maybe even a little repulsed—probably partially seeing my parents hungrily reach for it first at home growing up and me rolling my eyes over it, a rare moment of playful laughing together in the kitchen, so Dustin was overjoyed when I didn't fight him for it. And all of my cousins and aunties loved seeing his unabashed exuberance as he finished off the mango seed. And why wouldn't they—it wasn't uncommon for them to catch any errant trails of mango juice running down the length of their arms with a slow drag of their tongue, almost absent-mindedly, not wanting to waste a single drop. We saw people do that in restaurants and at picnics at the beach. This is a self-portrait. No one wants a drop to go to waste. The sweetness in that juice is to be caught.

Even fashion has caught on to inspiration from the mango. The paisley pattern, developed in India, is originally based on the shape of a mango. And not just in fashion. Americans have clamored for the very specific Alphonso variety, banned from the country since 2006 over initial fears about a small insect. After a safer treatment for these pests was found, it grew to be a quid pro quo between Harley-Davidson motorcycles and mangoes. President Bush said if India finally allowed Harleys to be sold in its competitive market for motorbikes, he'd allow Alphonso mangoes to be sold in America. And to the delight of my parents and hundreds of thousands of immigrants especially, the ban on Alphonso mangoes was lifted.

"What America will be getting is the King of Fruit, Indian masterpieces that are burnished like jewels, oozing sweet, complex flavors acquired after two millenniums of painstaking grafting," the cookbook writer Madhur Jaffrey described in the *New York Times*. "I can just see them arriving at the ports: hundreds of wide baskets lined with straw, the mangoes nestling in the center like eggs lolling in their nests," she said.

I am split; I am halved. There is no other way I want to be. In that understanding, I am whole. I would laugh in the face of anyone who tells me what is appropriate for delicate ears, delicate sensibilities, smallness of worlds. There is no disguising I am half South Asian, half Filipino, all-American. No desire to ever hide anymore. It has taken over forty years to figure it out (and I'm still learning!), but there is no hiding who I am anymore. My friends love me for all of me, and I have no more time or worry for anyone who needs me to hide my culture, my loves, what makes me happy.

While I was learning how to nourish and care for another while he was still forming inside of me, I offered up the fruit that was offered up to me by both of my parents when *they* found some (much to their delight) in a grocery store in the suburbs or small-town America. The fruit that was always offered up to me by my grandparents in India and the Philippines when they were still here walking among us.

And now I am the mother of two teen boys who fight over who gets to eat off the seed. Our shipment of Alphonso mangoes arrives tomorrow. Just in time for my youngest's thirteenth birthday celebrations. Mango for me will always signal such a heady memory of first becoming a mom, hearing the double heartbeat inside of me, the growing fists and feet signaling—yes yes, and *more*.

PAWPAW

f a bloom falls into your hand, someone might think stigmata—
the petals are *that* burgundy, the color of sweet sangria, or
that good blood you might get blossoming at your knee after a scrape from roller skates or racing too fast on your bike.
Your wheel catches a spot of sand near a curb and *bam*: a flower
at your elbow or at your chin. And from these dark blossoms—
one of the prettiest deep reds in my garden, second only to okra
flowers—come the creamiest fruit in September.

Even the Shawnee word for pawpaw is *ha'siminikiisfwa*, which
is also the word for the pawpaw moon that we see each September, the stuff of *Friday Night Lights* and college football, and
college looms over us in particular because my eldest is a junior.
Most likely his absence will be the first time any of our babies
will be away longer than a weekend. And that bedroom in our
house—once filled with the clicks of Lego bricks and crunchy
spills on a hardwood floor—now gone so quiet—suddenly splits
wide open and empty, like a dry mouth stopped midscream.

Legend has it pawpaws were one of George Washington's
favorite desserts, and I wonder which enslaved person was the
first to slice one open and slide out the seeds for the tongue that
carved out whole battle stratagems in his sleep. And what did
that servant dream of, and could they remember that dark color
in their dreams sometimes, and did that mean a happy dream or
one that woke them in a sweat?

Throughout almost two decades of knowing each other, my
friend Ross has asked me at least once a year if I know what a
pawpaw is. *Yes*, I tell him—sweetly the first few years, then I can
hear the lift in my voice, a tad bit less patient each time afterward. Of *course* I've known them ever since my high school and

college days in Ohio! Just before I finished grad school there, a giant pawpaw festival started up in 1999 in Athens. But he loves to tell me they are called the Indiana banana even though we both know that pawpaws are also called lots of other things: *wild banana, prairie banana, West Virginia banana, Kansas banana, Kentucky banana, Michigan banana, Missouri banana, the poor man's banana, Ozark banana,* and *banango.* My youngest used to call them *custard cups* when he was little.

A few years ago, my book of nature essays was chosen for the Indiana Humanities' One State / One Story program, and when they invited me back to Bloomington, where Ross teaches, I was thrilled that he would be my conversation partner for the event. Before our chat in front of a kind and attentive audience, Ross gifted me some pawpaws picked just that morning from his back-yard. He said he was going to ask me to eat one in front of every-body, knowing it'd be almost certainly a messy affair, but thought better of it when he saw that I showed up for the event in profes-sor mode: a new teal dress and pink metallic strappy sandals. As much as he teases me, he knows I have my limits. If I had eaten one in front of the audience, I surely would have had the leg-endary pawpaw juice—a golden mash-up of banana and mango and burnt honey—dribbling down my chin in front of a packed auditorium.

The pawpaw blooms are what's known in the botany world as *perfect*: each flower has both male and female structures, both stamens and carpels. Pawpaws aren't pollinated by bees, but they require pollen from another tree to develop into fruit. Because of this, if you think about planting a pawpaw tree, you need to have at least one other tree (preferably two more), planted no more than ten feet away. And so pawpaws were the first trees we planted in our new home, a couple of them bought while we were still very much in the swell of the pandemic.

After having a postage stamp–size yard, with two growing boys, we looked for a place where we could have an acre, a yard with old trees and plenty of space for new ones too. Space to run and throw a baseball. Room to garden. Pawpaws are an understory kind of tree, which means they are used to growing cool and green under the shade of other trees while they are young. Once they are a bit more mature, they can thrive in full sun.

Ross was tickled when I told him that I had just bought two new trees. I know it could still be another five years or so—give or take another college football season—before a burgundy blossom offers up a single fruit. Not one to hide his infectious enthusiasm, Ross told me we'd graft our trees together to make a new variety. One of Indiana, one of Mississippi, and then what we should call it? The Indisippi? A Missianna? Our nicknames for each other are Axolotl and LL Lentils. So: an axolentil tree?

On the days I miss my parents so much, when they tell me they are puttering around their backyard garden in Florida, I love sending them what I call Happy Mail. Examples: postcards from my sons about what they ate that week, a new sun hat for the garden, some nifty nail clippers made in Japan. Once, I found a family online that was selling pawpaws shipped in a box lined with straw: "*Fresh pawpaw fruit. 1 pound, plus you'll get to keep and plant the seeds from them.*" Turns out half of them would arrive black and overripe, but I wasn't worried. It's not like eating the too-sweet, too-gooey texture of an overripe banana. Even when pawpaws turn black, you can chill them in the fridge for a few hours, then scoop them out with a spoon to get to the "custard" with a bite of tartness, a small startle, like the light in late summer—the first bright afternoons of a new school year when the sun scatters and dapples your loved one's faces.

My sons have not graduated yet. They are still neck-deep in sports, clubs, youth group at church. We have taken care to limit how many extracurriculars they have so that we aren't driving all over town like chauffeurs. We can still enjoy one another at home. We can sit and read together on the back porch, until one of them nods off and I can smell their salt grass–scented heads fallen over onto my shoulder. And if you are around anyone still in school, you know how they all start to smell a little like erasers and freshly sharpened pencils. Or perhaps a marker smell so strong it chops and wrinkles your nose. And maybe you remember a year when you took your eldest to buy school supplies and he picked out everything blue or turquoise, because he probably knew those were *your* favorite colors, and that meant you'd probably get him just about anything he wanted if it was in that blue: a backpack with blue stars and solar systems, a blue pencil case, blue folders, a blue lunch bag with pawpaw-colored stripes. But he also wanted—and I said no to these—tiny vials of blue glitter, blue glue, bright markers with four different shades of blue, and, for some reason, blue thumbtacks and blue Post-its, even though he was six and had no idea what they were used for.

O let me time travel to any of those sweet years, let me say yes to him more often. Especially over the little things, like a pack of M&M'S on the checkout line. A tiny flashlight. O don't let him hold a grudge for all the hundreds of times I told him no. Let him remember as he's walking to and from his classes the thousands and thousands of times I told him *yes*. Maybe by the time he first comes home from college one weekend a few Septembers from now, we will have our earliest pawpaws to pick. Surely the dark-bloom will give forth a few creamy moons in our backyard. I know I will be so happy that we are four, four, four, FOUR again, that his room will be loud and full again, if only for the weekend. O if he comes home in September, the month when pawpaws sweeten up on trees all over the heart-shaped state of Ohio, or Indiana, and the Carolinas, into grassy Kentucky and Virginia, swooping into Missouri and Arkansas, winding around the verdant green of north Mississippi and Alabama, and looping up through the hills and mountains of Tennessee—

I promise I will let him have the first bite.

LUMPIA

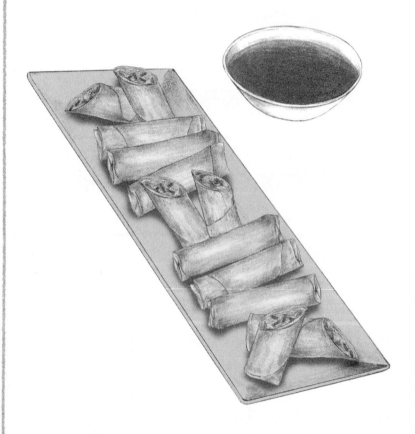

O n my fourteenth birthday, I didn't even want to have it on the table. My parents said I could have a sleepover and pizza, and we had access to eighties cable television, which meant movies like *The Legend of Billie Jean* or *The Lost Boys* or *The Goonies* playing on HBO. I was grinning while tidying up all day long. This was a big deal—it was huge, in fact. My immigrant parents were never fond of my spending the night at other people's houses, as they themselves never did such things when they were growing up, and I can imagine them wanting to protect my younger sister and me from all the dreadful shenanigans they had witnessed on sitcoms and movies of the time: Prank calls! Sneaking out to meet boys! Piercing ears with a needle! Smoking and drinking!

This is not an essay that stays small and embarrassed.

Things I wanted that year: pink-and-black British Knights hightops and Liz Claiborne perfume in the red triangle bottle. Both too, too audacious to wish for, cost-wise for my frugal parents, who watched over our small allowance: fancy high tops and perfume for a girl in junior high, no way! But commercials of both were on heavy rotation in the late eighties, and I even sketched out my hopes in colored pencil, casually leaving these elaborate sketches on the dining-room table before bed.

But even if I never got a single present on this birthday, I already felt so lucky: both parents were off from work; neither was even on call (which usually meant leaving before cake and presents and not coming home till the wee hours of the morning after racing back to the hospital for a patient emergency). I think back and realize my sister and I still had rooms right next door to each other. I loved that, sharing a wall we could tap-tap-tap in our own sister Morse code, instead of saying goodnight out loud and waking our parents. There was nothing more I could ask for.

This is not an essay that is ashamed.

One of the reasons this slumber party at our house was special and unconventional was because we lived on the psychiatric hospital grounds, right next to the patients' baseball stadium. My parents couldn't believe my friends' parents let their kids spend the night. But as my friend put it: *Aimee, my parents said it's the safest place in town! There's security cars and cameras all over the place!*

The other reason this was going to be a big deal was that there was going to be pizza. Capozzi's Pizzeria pizza, to be exact—the best in town, with its signature thick and spicy pepperonis, scattered and almost burnt every time. Every teen in town loved that pizza.

What I *didn't* know is that my mom had rolled three dozen lumpia the night before. Lumpia is a deep-fried finger food in the Philippines, made of a filling of chicken or ground beef, carrots, and green beans, and my mom puts raisins in for a hint of sweetness. Shanghai lumpia is rolled thinner and smaller and uses *giniling* (ground pork) and lettuce and diced garlic and shallots.

The filling is wrapped and folded into a small roll, a little thicker than my thumb, and these rolls are fried to a golden crisp with a piping hot filling inside and usually served with a sweet chili sauce for dipping. Even though I loved this party food so much, I told her no, we didn't *need* lumpia at a party. Pizza and cake and chips and two liters of pop was all we needed. We were going to spend the rest of the party choreographing dances, and remember—you promised to give us some space! *A party without lumpia!* was her astonished reply. *No. We don't do that. No. There will be lumpia!*

The thing is, for me, lumpia has always been synonymous with gatherings, with parties. I've always thought that, since before I could say a complete sentence, as there are pictures with me holding a single lumpia in my chubby fist, and I still think it even now. You know it's a true party when someone brings a tray of lumpia. Once my friends started trickling in on that snowy December night, mom started up the frypan to heat the canola oil for frying. I remember taking my friends' coats and wanting to hide and stay there in the coat closet. None of my friends had lumpia for their birthday, and even though it remains one of my very favorite finger foods, I just wanted it to be like everyone else's birthdays. I should have known the very fact that a fourteen-year-old was having a birthday sleepover at a mental asylum meant I'd never ever be like everyone else, so it would be pointless to pretend. Bite by bite, with each lumpia I ate with my friends that night, I should have known that, should have figured that out on my own.

This is a food essay that remembers jamboree.

I know how to roll the filling into thin powdered crepe-like wrappers. Moisten a fingertip in a small bowl of water and drag your wet finger around the edge of the V-shaped seal. Stick and wet your finger again for good measure on top of that seal so it doesn't burst apart in the hot oil like an exploded star in the night sky of your sizzling frypan.

I used to be embarrassed that I don't know how to make the filling exactly, though I've tried several times to get it to come close to my mother's sweet and savory blend and exquisitely tiny and even cuts (she's never used or wanted to use a food processor). But my husband of all people comes the closest to replicating my mother's recipe, so I am more than happy. He makes them for me when he knows I'm a little homesick for my mom. Or when our whole house could use some comfort food, usually in the dead of winter.

Until I was in second grade, we lived in Chicago, and my parents' Filipino friends and neighbors gathered pretty regularly for potlucks. The kids would scamper down to shag-carpeted basements to dance and play. I remember running up furry stairs to get fuel—lumpia, one in each hand—then running back downstairs so I wouldn't miss the next plottings and stratagems of a game of tag or Ghost in the Graveyard. Songs like "You Could Do Magic," by the band America, or "You Are the Woman," by Firefall, would be blasting, and soon the grown-ups would call us to come and dance in front of them. Woe to the Filipino child who did not want to dance, or worse, didn't like dancing at all.

Those are some of the dearest moments of my childhood: the exquisite glee and butterflies in my tummy while performing some rudimentary choreographed routine with a lumpia in each hand, like tiny batons for that little girl. And when the song was over, applause would erupt from the edges of the party, and then I'd bite and crunch all the lumpia I could. Why did I somehow forget that elation, those dances, when I was fourteen?

This is the apology of all apologies to my parents for ever being embarrassed of our food. My friends that did try something new—most of them for the first time—even finished theirs, some said, *Great job, Dr. Paz!* A couple of them wouldn't even try a bite, literally wrinkling their nose at the plateful my mom artfully stacked in a pretty pyramid. And that's when I got mad and instead of wanting to apologize that there was lumpia on the table of pizza and chips and dip, I thought of my mom taking the time off her busy schedule and the holiday prep to tenderly cut each carrot and bean. I remember this so well because that was the last time I ever felt shame about my food. Because in watching people who I considered dear pals not even *try* something so lovingly made with my mother's hands, I gained pride instead. I think I had just one slice of pizza. The rest of my meal was all lumpia.

Even now, when my mother hears we will be visiting her and my father in Florida, she will chop by hand all the ingredients for the lumpia filling, as she knows we are all hoping for a giant platter of them for at least one of our meals. Her grandsons love the crunch. Her son-in-law from Kansas loves the crunch. And most of all, her eldest daughter loves that crunch—it's the closest feeling to what it's like to have a room full of elders erupt into applause as you dance and twirl like you were six years old, one lumpia in each hand.

TOMATO

I f there is a better-smelling vegetable than a tomato grown in dirt and ripened in the sun, I don't know it. But I know I could almost conjure up that smell just from looking at my father's old Super 8 video home movies. I think a tomato is my first sensory memory, though I'm sure having the movie available to me as a kid helped amplify this remembrance.

One of my parents' favorite home movies of me takes place in their suburban Chicago house in the seventies. I was maybe two to three years old, trailing my mother, trying to get her attention while she worked out any stray weeds in their garden. The movie cuts, and we see my mother finally turn to me as I waddle over, this time holding a bevy of green tomatoes in the bucket of my dress, smiling and so proud: just like Mommy! Clearly she hadn't discovered the deliciousness of the green tomato like she has now. I can almost hear Mom's expletives in Tagalog, but can you blame me? I must have watched her pick red tomatoes all morning, and I've wanted to be just like her since I can remember: raven wavy hair, stylish clothes, even in the garden. What the camera doesn't show in *this* garden—their very first garden in a new country, all of time stretched out before her—is a question mark of when she will see her family in the Philippines again.

In the sixteenth century, the Spanish brought the tomato to the Philippines, and the Portuguese brought the tomato to India, and I—South Asian Filipina—planted my family's first tomato plants in north Mississippi in 2020. Along with thousands and thousands of people, we started tending to our gardens with a renewed sense of attention that year. We were home more often, so no more missed watering days, no excuses for letting our vegetables dry up. My husband and I had gardened together since we were first dating back in western New York, but this was to be a totally new plant hardiness zone: our first veggie garden in Mississippi.

The fear of tomatoes goes back hundreds of years. Folks in the Middle Ages thought tomatoes were poisonous, but that's only because they regularly ate them off pewter plates, which leached lead. In 1883, acrobat-performer John Ritchie was famously pelted with them after an audience disapproved of his performance, forcing him to flee the theater in a "perfect shower of tomatoes." As a kid, I remember funny, garish posters that screamed: "The nation is in chaos—can nothing stop this tomato onslaught?" This was the tag line for the 1978 movie *Attack of the Killer Tomatoes*, in which tomatoes lurked in corners and swimming pools waiting to harm Earth's citizens.

The Guinness Book of World Records notes that the largest-ever tomato plant grew in Epcot Center and produced over thirty-two thousand tomatoes, or over one thousand pounds of them, before it died in 2010. The gardeners pruned it as if it were a tree, with its stems utterly bare, no runners or leaves, until the umbrella of branches and fruit towered over twenty feet tall.

Food writers and cooks say the tomato represents umami flavor the best because its savory but sweet flavor comes from its high acid content. Soy sauce and fish sauce are all foods high in umami, so it's no surprise they pair deliciously with tomatoes too.

For my mother, the seeds have long been planted in her mind that the garden was a sort of shelter, perhaps a way to control and think about something else besides missing her own family. Her tiny mother (my Lola Felipa) remains frozen with a perpetual soft smile in the framed picture in our living room, already a ghost for three years by the time that gardening home movie was taken, as my mom lost her just a month after she gave birth to me during a hard winter in Chicago.

I think that ghost still travels across the ocean to her grand-daughter, and has been for over forty-nine years—this grand-daughter who skim-searches the face of every elderly Filipina that she encounters for a sweet and resigned smile just like in her mom's framed picture.

I write this song of tomatoes to my Lola and wonder if she would be amazed, if she would smile at my life, and what I've made with my husband and my own garden. What would the clicks of her tiny kitten heels on my paver stones sound like? And would those clicks rhyme with the bubbles of our birdbath? And would it make sense to her plumeria trees, back across the ocean and into the Philippines? Or would it be more like a joke she's too tired to ask my mother to translate, and would she just leave me with a tired chuckle, a pat on my hands while bringing them to her face so she could smell the tomatoes she never knew how to grow?

BANGUS

Filipino breakfast with bangus is so nice, you say it twice. The scientific name for bangus (milkfish) is *Chanos chanos*—one of my favorite tautonyms, in which the same word is used for both genus and species. Other favorites include *Chinchilla chinchilla, Chaos chaos, Pipa pipa, Vulpes vulpes,* and once I even swam in the middle of a school of *Boops boops* in the Aegean sea.

Bangus is the national fish of the Philippines. They have gorgeous silver flanks, a pale belly, and large eyes that can locate algae and wiggly invertebrates to nibble on, even in cloudy coral reefs. On average they are about fifteen inches long, almost the length of a bowling pin. And when they get spooked or need to escape a predator, they can leap out of the water and "fly."

My favorite way to prepare bangus is deep fried after soaking in a marinade of ginger and vinegar. Filipino breakfast for me means bangus, garlic fried rice, and fried egg with the yolk just a tad runny: *bangusilog!* And you can't forget diced, salt-and-peppered tomatoes on the side. For a *sobremesa*, when the main food is finished but conversations keep going—sliced mangoes or some stone fruit finish it off. For years, this kind of breakfast meant my mother and I were waking up in the same house. Now that we aren't under the same roof anymore, and I have a family of my own, I cherish those times my parents gather at the breakfast table with us even more. And if I'm somehow having Filipino breakfast in the world without my mom at the table, it's because I'm at a table with people who love and honor the Filipino side of my heart. The ones with whom I never have to hold in my loud, table-slapping laughter-cackles. The ones who make me leap with joy when I see their names on my phone or get a postcard in the mail from them. Who are the first to RSVP to my wedding, buy my latest book, send a sweet gift for my babies when I tell them I'm pregnant. The first to call after a breakup. Or drama at work. *The ride-or-dies.* Filipino breakfast means a party on the tabletop and a jamboree in my heart when I finally stand up from the meal. My friend Joseph says bangus is smoky and unctuous. Flaky light oiliness that melts into umami. Simms, my thirteen-year-old foodie pal in Jackson, Mississippi, also says bangus is smoky, salty, dry, and mild—golden-crispy. Best with salted tomatoes and rice.

The inner flavor of bangus is indeed kissed with smoke and lightly soused. When pan-fried, it gives a delightfully sharp crunch before you get to the flaky white fillet. When I eat bangus it makes me feel like I am flying—over the Delta, and good morning across the Gulf of Mexico, spilling into the Pacific, then swooping low over the Philippine Sea, and skimming the surface of the China Sea, just off the coast of Bolinao, the province in northern Philippines where my Kuya once helped run a bangus business, an aquaculture, fish pens and fish pens of them. Bangus is the fish that makes me feel as if I am flying toward something like home. But maybe the grandfish of those bangus that have since been released from those pens are flying somewhere nearby, too, just waiting for me to visit them, waiting for me to test out these wings.

RICE

n sixth grade, my friends and I wanted our own jar of rubber cement, but no one we knew actually owned one, except for our teacher. For class projects, we were all expected to have our own bottle of drippy white glue or, worse yet, Elmer's paste in a plastic can that you'd have to spread on thick with that gummy plastic spatula attached to the lid. That paste always dried out so quickly that most any project with construction paper ended with a few globs of paste hidden under paper like several hamsters trapped under a rug because of overzealous paste spreading.

Asking for school supplies that weren't on the list was out of the question for my parents, who thought school supplies were already superfluous. "We have pen here! Look, I have notebooks from work! Good enough for me, good enough for you!" It's not that I was above using free stuff, but they failed to understand that I was hesitant to use them because the free pens and note-pads from the hospital were emblazoned with prescription drug names. Since my mom was a psychiatrist, my school supplies had names like Prozac, Haldol, and Depakote emblazoned on them. How I longed for good ol' Bic or Paper Mate pens. Or the crème de la crème of all pens: the four-colored jumbo pen where one click of a button could summon what seemed like such an ex-travagant choice of ink colors: red, black, blue, and green. When I cringed at these office supply "freebies" my parents brought home from work, my mother would call out that if I didn't like it, I could just "use rice!"

To "use rice" was not a metaphor, it was literal—my mom loved to regale me with stories from the Philippines about how the sari-sari store in their province, where they usually bought all their supplies, didn't carry glue for envelopes or wrapping paper when she was growing up. They simply used cooked rice instead—spreading it with their fingers like a thin paste, one grain at a time. Suddenly my Prozac notebook didn't look so bad anymore!

This glue is famously strong—even the Great Wall of China is held together with sticky rice. Sort of: while the Great Wall was being built in the fifteenth and sixteenth centuries, workers used a porridge made of calcium carbonate and rice as a mortar to hold the wall's stones together. But rice is a very thirsty plant to farm—five thousand liters of water are needed to produce about two pounds of rice. In the United States, most of the rice farming is done on family farms across the states of Mississippi, Arkansas, California, Louisiana, Missouri, and Texas.

The three types of rice refer to the length and width of rice grains after they're cooked. Long grain's kernels are over four times as long as they are wide when cooked. The grains stay separate and fluffy like in jasmine and basmati rice, my favorite. Medium grains have a short and wide kernel with a slightly sticky consistency after it's cooked, like in arborio rice. And sushi rice is a good example of short grains, whose kernels are about twice as long as they are wide; this makes for the stickiest type of texture when cooked. There are more than forty thousand varieties of rice in the world, and it is grown on every continent except Antarctica. Americans eat more than twenty-six pounds of rice every year. That might seem like a lot, but it's nothing compared to the rest of the world. According to the US Rice Producers Association, people in Asia eat up to three hundred pounds a year, and residents of the United Arab Emirates consume four hundred fifty pounds per year. The French, on the other hand, eat hardly any rice at all—just ten pounds every year.

The Banaue Rice Terraces in the Philippines are one of the wonders of the world and look like grand emerald staircases leading up to the clouds—fitting, as rice is the staple food of the

Filipinos and revered as bounty on so many tables. Rice is adaptable, easy to grow (provided there is a good water source), and has a very high production yield—just one seed of rice can result in over three thousand grains. When I was little, one of the first things my mom taught me how to use was a rice cooker, ubiquitous in every Filipino household. When she was in a particularly good mood, I could hear her sing out this famous Filipino kids' song from the kitchen as she cooked:

Planting rice is never fun, bent from morn to set of sun;
Cannot stand and cannot sit; cannot rest a little bit.
Oh, my back is like to break; oh, my bones with dampness ache,
And my legs are numb and set from the soaking in the wet.

When the sun begins to break, you will wonder as you wake
In what muddy neighborhood there is work and pleasant food?
It is hard to be so poor and such sore and pain endure.
You must move your arms about or you'll find you'll be without.

Ironic that the song recalls how tedious this manual labor is, to the point of wrecking a body. More often than not, she sounded so happy when she sang and cooked for us when she was home and not on call at the hospital.

What a wonder. I think of her every time I'm in the kitchen feeling a little harried during the week. She truly made it seem like there was nothing more she wanted to do besides be in the kitchen and cook for us. And for the times I asked to help, she always scooted me off to play outside or do homework, or "rest up." As a mother myself now, I barely feel like cooking on days I come home from teaching all day, and take turns with my husband on days when he doesn't teach. Our jobs aren't nearly as stressful as hers was, so her generosity and merriment seem extraordinary, especially after being with mentally ill patients who could often be belligerent to her at work.

And if I was close enough to hear her planting rice song, that means I was probably watching TV in the next room or probably, I'm embarrassed to admit, possibly even growing annoyed because I couldn't hear *Scooby-Doo* or *Voltron* clearly thanks to her singing. I marvel over her sad song, sung with a happy tone. What did it mean that she sang it happily when she could have been resting and not chopping veggies for lumpia, or making us chicken adobo?

The one thing my mother let me do ever since I was a little girl was to wash the rice, measure water using the ring-finger method taught to her by my Lola Felipa, and set the rice up in our rice cooker. When I wash and measure rice in my own kitchen, I can hear her call out *"Magsaing ka na!"* (cook the rice now), like she did when I was a teenager at home. Every Pinoy knows this easy trick to get the perfect amount of water for cooking rice. Once you learn how to do it, you'll never look back:

Dip the tip of your fingers straight down into the pot until they just touch the rice, and add more water until it reaches the first joint-line of your ring finger. I was dubious, but Mom said, *Trust me—we have been doing this for years and years.* It doesn't seem like this method would be effective, given all the different sizes of hands, but it turns out the distance of the tip of your ring finger to the first knuckle is relatively similar for everyone. Why does the knuckle method work? Assume you're using your favorite rice-cooking pot. The volume of water between the top of the rice and your first knuckle is always the same.

I barely knew any Filipinos growing up that weren't related, but now that my inner circle, my *barkada*, all like to cook, I still giggle that we all know this finger measure method even though we all grew up like scattered rice across the country: Los Angeles,

Oregon, New Jersey, Virginia, Ohio. I have no proof other than the fact that their children live to toast one another and regularly schedule meals together, almost always involving rice. It is a reunion of our chosen family that feels safe and familiar, comforting. But I have a gut feeling that our moms and dads who taught us that rice measuring trick would all have been good *prens* in another life, with their giant laughs, the clapping of hands, and the pounding of tables during an especially funny joke one of them cracked. At this imaginary table of my dreams, I'd be willing to bet there would be several neatly mounded bowls of rice—all perfectly cooked, never too mushy or too dry—scooped in beautiful ceramics, still piping hot, steaming puffs of little clouds into the air.

PINEAPPLE

Spring brings the boom-burst of new life, of pineapples and hummingbirds throughout most of the world. On the island of Oahu, red cayenne pineapples ripen to reveal their signature golden flesh, and sugarloaf pineapples glow pale, almost white, when they are ready to pick. Hummingbirds show up in every state in America except Hawaii—their tiny wings can't make the long distance to the archipelago and survive strong oceanic winds. But even if they could survive the long flight across the ocean, hummingbirds are officially forbidden as imports into the state because they pollinate pineapples, which renders the fruit less marketable as the flesh becomes riddled with pebble-like seeds.

When I was pregnant with my eldest son, we passed his due date by two full weeks in late May, just as strawberries began to plump and ripen. I tried every home remedy I could to induce labor naturally, but nothing worked. I remember slowly waddling my way around the block with my husband, carrying a fork in hand while Dustin held a bright red bowl of cut pineapple pieces—because more than a few friends suggested it would make the baby come quicker. I'd take a few steps, then stab one of the juicy pieces. Step-step, stab. Step-step, stab. I had never had a whole meal of pineapple—more pineapple than I had eaten in more than a decade in just that one walk around the block.

Maybe it was a coincidence, but that very next morning, my spring child was finally born and answered my call—round and full of sweetness from the start. One autumn evening five years later, I was finishing up his bedtime routine (milk, bath, book, songs) and was about to leave his room when he said, "Oh, Mommy! I forgot to tell you something!" I sat at the edge of his bed, expecting one more goodnight, one more kiss, his usual delay tactics at the time. Or maybe another blanket—did I mention there was a lake-effect snow falling that night? I leaned my face close to his, and he whispered, "I forgot I'm supposed to bring three pineapples to school tomorrow!"

My face squinched up in confusion. Apparently, this was for his kindergarten's annual "Sharing Feast" for Thanksgiving, but this was the first I'd heard of it. The students were supposed to bring in their favorite food to share with the class. Everyone else had volunteered for things like cupcakes, cookies, and various chips, but my son had promised his classmates not just one, but three pineapples—his favorite fruit. My husband came in, asked us to repeat what was going on, and saw our child and his giant, hopeful eyes bubbling over with pineapple fever. The next thing I knew, Dustin was hitching up his snow pants and pulling on his boots to make a slow and steady drive to our local grocery store in the evening blizzard.

These days, when my parents visit us from central Florida, they bring crowns of pineapples from their yard and ask for jars of water to set them in before they even hug me hello. The French priest Father Du Tertre called pineapples "the king of fruits because it wears a crown." This new round of crowns on the kitchen windowsill stretches a fresh beard of watery roots. We won't see one of the actual tiny, softball-size fruits for three years or so, but after a long, hard winter, I'm grateful for this pineapple jamboree on my sill, and the frenzy and frolic of new growth.

ONION

Among the ingredients in one of the world's oldest cookbooks were onions, most probably grown in Central Asia, according to the cuneiform from Babylonian tablets. *Allium* genus and the word *onion* means: large pearl.

Biennial and botanical variations of onions are shallots shushing one another.

Cold feet are a thing of the past if there's a spare onion around—a rub of a halved onion on your freezing toes is all you need to get your blood warming like a soup again.

Desperate to get rid of the smell of paint from a newly decorated room? Place a sliced onion on a table.

England used to believe it customary to throw an onion after a bride as a means of warding off the Evil Eye.

French onion soup folklore says the origins of this soup go to King Louis XV retiring to his hunting lodge late at night and finding nothing but onions, butter, and champagne in his pantry and asking his cook to figure something out. Modern versions now add a heavy dose of grated cheese on top of the soup and then set it under the broiler for what is known as the classic Gratinée des Halles.

Guinea pigs and dogs shouldn't nibble on these; onions are pure poison for them.

A Hippocrene of hundreds of writers is to use the onion as a metaphor to describe the layers and layers of plot, a character, or even a stanza, and here I am, joining them, with glee.

In India, the onion was supposed to ward off plague if you hung a strand of them near the entrance to your house. Colonizers thought this to be one of India's silly customs of superstition, but a terrible outbreak of plague arrived and the natives who hung the onions outside their homes escaped the pandemic, while others died off like flies, crispy and shriveled.

Juice of an onion can be rubbed on athletes' sore muscles to help keep them warm and supple.

The King of the Onions was a man who held the entire onion world hostage and made a fortune from his shady onion stockpiling of nine million onions, in warehouses in Chicago, and after flooding the market with ultracheap onions, caused many onion farmers to go bankrupt. Because of this, Eisenhower signed the Onion Futures Act in 1958, which makes it illegal to trade onion futures in America—the only agricultural product that is specifically outlawed.

Love charm: Take four, five, or eight onions, name them after your crushes, and place them near the chimney; the first that sprouts will be your true love.

Mincing onions means cutting them as small as you can. If you cry while cutting onions like I do, place them in the freezer for about fifteen to twenty minutes. Then, lay one hand flat across the tip of your knife and use a rocking motion to chop. Keep going until the onions reach an evenly sized fine dice, as small as grains of rice if you can. Be sure to hold down the tip of the knife, otherwise the onions will fly around the room, tiny birds zipping around your kitchen, looking for the closest window.

News from *The Onion*, a satirical newspaper, often gets mistaken for bona fide real events taking place. On some of these wild and wacky days, even I get confused.

Onion's skin very thin—mild winter's coming in.

Pedanius Dioscorides is the ancient Greek physician known as the "Father of Medicinal Plants." He advised preparing athletes for Olympic games by eating pounds of onions, drinking onion juice, and rubbing sliced onions on their bodies to warm their muscles.

Quantities of onions appearing in your dreams means prepare for all the spite and envy from people by being successful. But if you eat the onions in your dream, you will nip all their bitter hearts at the root and their jealousy won't cream. If you see dream onions still growing, sweetening, pearling, until they fill the room you dream in, there will be just enough rivalry in your affairs to make your days simmer.

Riza Pasha, minister of war in the Ottoman Army to Abdul Hamid, kept "a string of large onions at one side of his mantelpiece as a defense against the Evil Eye."

Satan stepped out of the Garden of Eden after the Fall of Man, onions sprang up from the spot where he placed his right foot, and garlic from where his left foot touched. If an onion's skin is

Thick and tough—coming winter cold and rough.

An **U**mbel of an onion is made up of white teeny flowers on top of short flower stalks that emerge from a common base, like the ribs of an umbrella.

Vidalia onions need to be harvested by hand and they won't make you cry. This sweet onion needs particular soil and can only be grown in southeast Georgia to achieve that sweet and crisp crunch without any of the acidity of other onions.

Wise Egyptians worshipped the onion, believing that its spherical shape and concentric rings symbolized eternal life.

X-rays might show concentric circles of new layers of bone growing. This pattern resembles the layers of an onion, and when this happens it is called an *onion skin periosteal reaction.*

Y-shaped hollow and tubular green stems poke out of my garden to wave hello as we head back to school each August—the boys to middle and high school, Dustin and me back on campus to teach, all of us lambent with a light sheen of sweat.

Zebra onion grass is often used for colorful reptile backgrounds and for greenery in interior design. It's an invasive cousin to onion, and the small purple flowers startle people when they turn up in their lawns before they blast them with some herbicide that kills them but also kills any number of bugs and crawlies, which means less food for birds, and it definitely kills fireflies, too, and what does this mean when just since my last book was published in 2020, there've been even fewer fireflies, and meanwhile my sweet neighbors keep spraying poison and even waving while doing so sometimes, and my husband and I keep planting pollinators and native grasses and offering up cups of birdseed hung from our trees, and I wonder about the drift from the herbicide spray from both sides of our property, how those green Ys of our onions that we pick and feed to our children and our friends, and my parents and your parents, all these onions must have the faintest spray from the drift, the drift, O what about that *drift*?

LYCHEE

n 2023, a lychee tree over a thousand years old popped to life again after locals thought it was all but dead. In China's Sichuan province, that tree was determined to have been planted in the Tang dynasty (618–901). This tree is about fifty feet tall—as tall as if sixteen giant pandas stood on each other's shoulders. No one knows why it erupted, heavily dotted with fruit again, but the locals are thrilled. The last time it bore its fruit—with signature tough-red warty skin and a translucent milk-white dome of flesh inside the hard casing—was 2012.

What's inside a lychee bounces us glimmer-glimmer and lusters lamplight into moonlight on our walls and floor. Sometimes I think heaven must be made of it—every window, chair, pale leaves juddering on every tree, every shimmered open door.

One of the most beloved concubines of Emperor Zhong had a penchant for the fruit. She adored it so, the emperor had couriers ride over twelve hundred miles to fetch some for her in the capital. No surprise, then, that the lychee, or "Chinese strawberry," is a symbol of love and romance. Each fruit is about the size of a golf ball, but it can be oval or even heart-shaped too.

When I first met Joseph Legaspi and Sarah Gambito, Filipino writers close to my own age, they were on the cusp of forming Kundiman, an Asian American writing organization. One of their earliest ventures was a poetry reading series at the bar Verlaine in Manhattan, where the signature drink was a lychee martini. The lychee martini was cold and crisp, with a tart and light sweetness. It was the first time in my adulthood I heard the phrase "signature drink," and that phrase signed itself in my heart. Even now, lychees and iced Nuoc Trai Vai drinks from Vietnamese restaurants always remind me of this friendship with Joseph and Sarah that I cherish with all my heart.

I lived in western New York in the early 2000s and this was before I was married with kids, so catching an eighty-eight-dollar flight to the city was fairly easy. I could go from Buffalo to JFK in just under an hour. I could go from being in a sea of small-town whiteness to another kind of family in the city, all of us tumbled and unattached in our twenties, but forming into gemstones I still treasure over two decades later. Instead of agate, jasper, lapis lazuli, sodalite, obsidian, quartz—I had Joseph, Sarah, Pat, Vikas, Lara, Oliver, Jon, Ron, and more.

Sometimes, I'd get a paper sack full of lychees from the Union Square Market and sit on a bench and shell them into a neat pile of red rinds. To open up a lychee, you can use your hands—the red exocarp will give way with a little pressure from your thumb-nail. Once you've broken the skin, you can peel it away and pop the whole white syrupy aril into your mouth and chew lightly—be mindful of the almond-size dark seed at the center.

I'd carefully peel my lychees and watch the people in the city walk and rush by, people I thought had Very Important Lives to scurry home to. Where there might be a partner waiting, kids crawling to the door to greet them. All of which I didn't have at the time, but I held so much hope in my small beating red heart that I might—one day. Maybe a house, two kids? Three? Maybe there would be space for a garden, enough to plant a small tree together, and we could say years later, *I remember when we first planted this tree, our family was just beginning . . .*

Oh, but I was a brand-new English professor then, and there didn't seem to be any time or space or place for me in that teeny town to even whisper that dream aloud. But I still felt so lucky, so alive, during my visits—I had a sack of lychees, and I had sunshine in Union Square. In Washington Square some days. In

Bryant Park some days. I had friends who made my heart leap. A different kind of family of Asian American writer pals, still growing, strengthening, all of us trying to make our way into the publishing world, eking out poems and sending them off to try and get published, slowly, but steadily. I still can't fully explain how we all immediately felt like long-lost cousins who finally reunited in both the quiet and loud spaces among skyscrapers and subway lines. A few lychee martinis here and there. And loads and loads of laughter after various poetry readings in the city together. A different kind of treasure.

MINT

Can I find any lasting solace in the color green?
    —"Mint Snowball," Naomi Shihab Nye

You can smell it before you spot it, one of the first fragrant greetings of spring. Even if it looks like the stems have turned black and the leaves are brown and crispy during the dreary winter months, it's one of the hardiest herbs in the country—its Kelly-green, aromatic leaves unfurl and sprout year after year. Mint is also known as the herb of hospitality, perfect for friends who say they can't keep any plant alive. The roots are called runners for a reason—the stolons, their square and horizonal stems, are easy and eager to spread. Once you invite mint into your garden, it simply will not leave.

If you pick the leaves just before it flowers, you'll have mint in abundance from spring until the first frost. Some varieties will grow up to five feet tall in that time, whereas others will stay wee and fairylike, with leaves as tiny as a typed letter *o*. The flowers are labiate—the blossom has a distinctive upper and lower lip, parted just so, as if the bloom itself is exhaling the cool arctic blast we get if we pop a mint candy on our tongues.

In literature, mint is found in Shakespeare, Chaucer, and even the Bible. In Greek mythology, Minthe was a nymph who had an affair with Hades, and when Persephone discovered this, she trampled her to the ground, turning her into a plant. But the more she stomped, the more fragrant was the air. Ancient Athenians used mint to scent their arms, the smell a poignant remembrance of an embrace. Now it scents the air in hospitals: in waiting rooms, to keep awake those waiting for news of their loved ones, and in operating rooms, where a few drops of peppermint oil can keep corporeal smells at bay. Hot peppermint tea is still the go-to for sniffles and coughs.

In the language of flowers, mint means "your personality is *refreshing*." Bees love the smell, but houseflies, mice, aphids, and mosquitoes all scurry and fly away from it. In the language of my youth, it will always remind me of Wrigley's Spearmint gum, the only kind my mother kept in her purse. Mint will always mean *mother* for me, a doctor who kept things spotless and clean, and whose white lab coat and fancy dresses always smelled of Elizabeth Taylor's Passion perfume—and mint.

I can remember my mother passing me a stick of gum at the zoo or in a church pew before the choir started up their Sunday greeting. I remember how people stared at us when we walked into a sea of white faces at church, and how they stared even more at her trays of delicious lumpia or pancit noodles among all the unseasoned casseroles for potlucks after the service. But she taught me how to snap my gum, and the way her elegant jaw moved while chewing silently among the stares is a minty coolness I'll never be able to re-create. I haven't seen her in months, and it turns out I can't write about gardens and mint without thinking of her embrace. I can smell her hugging me if I close my eyes. She's the one who taught me how to garden, how to get my hands in the soil after the first frost, and when to prune and pull up errant growth. No wonder I'm a runner now, stretching for her light, for her smell, for her reviving embrace.

JACKFRUIT

The whole family gathered around when my grandfather placed *Manorama* newspapers on the dining table to slice a jackfruit open. He made sure I had a front-row seat at the opening. I mean I was at his elbow with that giant knife doing its good work, slicing open the pebbly rind to reveal the light yellow petals filled with a juice sweeter than I'd ever tasted before or since. The fruit was room temperature—too big to fit in any home refrigerator in town, but I didn't care. All I knew was my grandfather lifted a yellow bulb—like the head of a golden tulip—and I nibbled it down like a hungry chipmunk, and the whole gathering of neighbors and extended relatives who came to watch his American granddaughter try jackfruit laughed and laughed at my enthusiasm.

Jackfruit cold, Jackfruit cold and crunch, jackfruit sliced with a knife rubbed down with olive oil so it doesn't stick on the sweet flesh, jackfruit large and sun-split. My favorite fruit is the only thing that balms me now. It is raining cats and rats here in Florida for a beach vacation we'd planned for months, but my father just set a bowlful of fresh slices in front of me and suddenly there is only sun. And yet.

Because I've written about fruit for over twenty years, I often get asked what is my favorite fruit of all. I say my response so quickly, like a double bullet, a double bite, a double sting, that most people flinch at my enthusiasm. And the answer still hasn't changed ever since I first tasted one during my first visit to my grandparents' home in Kerala. *Jackfruit. Jackfruit.* The word *jackfruit* comes from Portuguese *jaca,* which in turn is derived from the Malayalam word for this fruit, *jakka.* I loved hearing my grandparents say the word as a question. They waited eight years before they could see their eldest grandchild for the first time, and there wasn't a single fruit or sweet they wouldn't give me. But it was Kerala's bounty of fruit—mangoes, plantain, jackfruit—a trifecta of abundance and juice that tasted like a coastal sunrise—that I was drawn to since the third grade during my first visit to India.

The fruit can grow up to three feet long and eighteen inches wide. The surface is covered with blunt thornlike ridges, which will soften as the fruit ripens. The bark on jackfruit trees produces an orange color used to dye monks' robes. In one year, a tree can produce up to two hundred fifty fruits—it's quite the sight, often stopping people in their tracks to see a tree with even fifty or so of them hanging there, daring to fall and split open, a sight not unlike the alien cocoons in the 1980s sci-fi movie *Cocoon*, which gave the humans who found them a renewed vim and vigor in their step.

When clusters of them dangle in the trees so high any one of them could injure me permanently if they fall—even one, since some jackfruit can weigh over a hundred pounds—well, it makes it seem like I'm walking under a tree full of dark leopards. As in, *You are here/there, all around me, above me.* It's the heaviest fruit in the world. A single jackfruit that my grandfather brought home was heavier than me and my younger sister combined!

What a curiosity I must have been to them—wearing shorts and not dresses, and my hair cut at my neck in a lightly feathered bob instead of long braids as was customary for girls my age in Kerala. I had eyeglasses too, plastic and pink: "Too much reading, reading, that one!" I overheard as my mother seemed to be apologizing to them after dinner, when all the kids left the table. There was no American pop music to be found on the television at that time, in the peak MTV years, so no Cyndi Lauper or Prince, but my sister and I had fun and dramatic Malayalam soap operas to giggle over instead each night, to wind down after a day spent exploring the pineapple and rubber-tree-filled plot of land full of spotted cuckoos, green bee eaters, and cobras that was our grandparents' backyard.

And relatives loved watching us watch TV, trying to understand plots that they'd explain to us, eight- and seven-year-old girls from America. What a curiosity my mother must have been to them too: a Filipina ten years their eldest son's senior, a doctor who would never be a stay-at-home wife, and Methodist to their Roman Catholic son to boot!

The jackfruit rinsed us clean of any worry about how we'd be treated in this country that felt familiar and unfamiliar to me. Upon seeing and hearing how much his granddaughter loved jackfruit, the neighbors across the street, who had a house elephant happily noshing sugarcane in their front yard, brought us a small mountain of them and left them at the entrance to my grandparents' outdoor kitchen. I couldn't believe this bounty of chartreuse ovals ready to be doled out for the next week of our visit. Such an auspicious welcome and bit of sweet kindness that didn't require any translation at all.

Almost forty years later, my grandparents have passed on, and the rain has finally stopped here in Florida as we are visiting my parents and hoping to salvage part of our vacation outdoors. But as I sit with my husband and boys around the dinner table, eating freshly cut jackfruit from my father, I don't mention my sweet memory of *his* father first doing the same thing for me when I was eight all those years ago, for fear that his knees might buckle just a little bit at the mention of the father he still misses so much. Whose absence still feels so fresh, you'd never guess we lost my grandfather over thirty years ago.

But I'm remembering now, I want to say to him, *and I never forgot,* and I'm telling him again and again, and the whole world, that I will *never* forget my grandfather, or my first taste of jackfruit from the man who took the time to type aerogrammes to me when I was in elementary school and sent those thin blue envelopes flying over to my side of the planet ever since I could read. I now have his typewriter in a glass case in our home and take it out to type letters to my own beloveds. Another remembrance of my grandfather reaching out to me, before he ever saw my bespectacled face in person smiling up at him, cheeks full of jackfruit.

CINNAMON

The holidays and this colder time of year find my kitchen in mostly happy chaos. With sporty teen boys home on winter break (and me having grown up just with a younger sister at home), no one—I mean, no one—prepared me for how much boys can eat! So there is much baking, spilling, stirring, and whirring—and the scent of cinnamon in my hands, my hair, even onto my sons' cheeks, which makes it seem like we must live under an invisible cloud of it in winter.

We get cinnamon from the Greek word *kinnámōmon*, meaning "sweet wood." This spice is one that has been documented as filling cavities of mummies in Egypt since 3000 BC, and was even mentioned in the Old Testament. For years, spice traders kept secret exactly where cinnamon could be found. Aristotle, in his *Historia Animalium*, claimed the spice came from the fragrant twigs of the nests of giant birds, which were cruelly toppled and shaken down to collect the fragrant sticks.

As much as I adore the story of giant "cinnamon birds" flying around and building massive nests, cinnamon actually comes from a tree in the laurel family. It's sustainable even after centuries of harvest in Sri Lanka and in the southern state of Kerala, India, where my father was born. My grandmother had a tree on her property, and I remember how it shook in the wind in anticipation of a monsoon. The cinnamon tree thrives with lots of rain, producing yellow flowers that give way to a sprinkle of violet berries. But it's not the berry from this tree that is harvested— the *bark* is the spice. The brownish paper-bag outer bark of the cinnamon trees is stripped, and then the inner bark is loosened, peeled carefully, and rolled into curls (quills) as it dries. True cinnamon sticks roll into multiple thin layers of bark. If your spice stick has one main curl, it's technically called *cassia*, redder in color and just a tad more bitter than true cinnamon.

There's an old ritual of blowing a pinch of cinnamon from your hand while you stand in a doorway, ideally under a new moon or on the first of the month. You stand in the doorway and blow a small poof of it to conjure up abundance and prosperity for your house. Prosperity for me means a wish for all (who want one) to have a doorway of their own, to find (or smell) a cloud of cinnamon when you and your loved ones walk through that door. I want cinnamon mulled in tea or cider after a long day for everyone who feels a little lonesome, a little too tired from so much work these days. Who is feeling cold and can't afford to turn up the heater too much more. So on the next first of the month, I will try to remember this fragrant ritual at our front door. And maybe I will blow a tiny bit of cinnamon for another door—for the ghosts of our loved ones to walk through. Let's welcome them all in, make them feel at home again.

APPLE BANANA

had almost forgotten about their twinned taste until my friend Kim, a writer and devoted protector of native birds on the island of Kauai, plopped a bag full of apple bananas on the counter, freshly plucked that morning from her garden. There are over a thousand banana varieties, and there was no way she could have known this, but apple bananas are my favorite. She was off to check on some albatross nests while I was staying at her friend's house, researching and writing with Dustin.

Our fifteenth anniversary trip was twice delayed, and before that, we hadn't gone away together for anything that wasn't work or a conference in about six years. Otherwise, we actually liked and preferred spending time with our boys, bringing them around the world with us. But this can be true too: you can like and want to spend time with your kids *and* you can also want to have some alone time with your partner or best friend. Those two feelings, contrary to what television and social media tells you, are not mutually exclusive. During this time away, the boys were home in Mississippi with Dustin's parents, who graciously drove all the way down from Kansas to make this happen. As someone who did not get to spend much time with grandparents, this was especially important and special to me—that they knew both sets of grandparents, so that helped me feel less guilty for leaving our boys behind.

So we said yes to the trip, a *Yes!* to Hawaii in January before campus opened up again—something wild and decadent and quietly much needed for the two of us. I knew—but maybe almost forgot in our day-to-day chauffeuring and getting the boys to dentist appointments and baseball and piano and and and—just how fun it was to *talk* to each other, and uninterrupted(!) for many

many minutes. Such novelty! How lovely to admire the green in Dustin's eyes again, green as the lightest parts of the Hīhīmanu mountain, my favorite mountain on the island because of its twin-peak shape that looks like a stingray rising into the sky on the left green arm of Hanalei Bay.

One bite of an apple banana and suddenly the signature double taste of them becomes a party in your mouth featuring a banana host and a sort of pineapple-strawberry DJ spinning tunes. Apple bananas seem to also taste like flowers—plumeria, maybe—so it's no surprise they are related to ginger plants and the bird-of-paradise flower. This banana is firmer than what we are used to in the States, the longer Cavendish banana, and on the apple banana, there's an echo of color calling out the faintest whisper of pink. The name *apple banana* is the general term for the tundan, silk, and manzano bananas—all short kings of the banana world, just four to five inches long, with this bright and fruity smell that hits you even with just the first strip of the skin peeled down.

The apple banana is believed to have originated in the Philippines, where they grow in abundance, and they also thrive in Southeast Asia and South America and some parts of Florida, which is where I last had one with my folks—in Homestead, Florida. Because of their smaller size, apple bananas are perfect for hiking, as they take longer to brown than the Cavendish ones. And that is just what we did. That week we took morning and sunset walks along the bay front, laughing at the goofy red-crested cardinals—"upside-down cardinals," we called them—because their heads are a flaming tomato red and their bellies look like there are wearing distinguished gray-and-white suits. We admired the young, fearless surfers—some looked just barely in school and that made us miss our boys.

But the scent of apple bananas reminds me to slow down, to

take that trip, to be intentional and present with my loved ones. To not take my sweet and chaotic dailyness for granted. What is it about scents that can make us stop in our tracks if we catch a whiff of them and bring us back to a moment we can return to again and again if need be? We are long gone from that meaningful time on the island, and college applications loom ever closer now for my eldest—but if I close my eyes when I'm in line at, say, the grocery or the post office back home, I can conjure up that giant stingray mountain, that exact smell of an apple banana, its creamy citrus swimming alongside me while I run errands.

The hīhīmanu have wingspans of six to ten feet, and their fin-wings wave unhurried and graceful in the north Pacific. When I bite into an apple banana, I am reminded of rest, of slowing down—and how good it is, and how we should try to help others get rest too: heart rest, eye rest, and mind rest. For me that means more slow walks and slow talks with Dustin. I remember that one spot on the beach by the lifeguard stand—the one spot where I once thought the sky above us was nothing but a dark expanse, but after a little bit of patience and training my eyes to notice again, what an emergence, of course they were there all along: thousands and thousands of stars.

MANGOSTEEN

O f course I felt guilty because a rare January ice storm was brewing back home in north Mississippi, while Dustin and I were in flip-flops, waiting in line at the Kauai fruit market for the chance to taste my first mangosteen. But my dear in-laws had once again assured us, comforted us, encouraged us to *Go! Go! Have fun!*, that they happily had everything under control, which included pancake plans and homemade cookies only a grandma could make with the boys, trips to the store for "snacks," and probably some toys too.

Dustin and I brought a brown paper sack of this precious fruit back to the home in Hanalei Bay where we were staying. The mangosteen looks like a purple persimmon. But the exocarp is rock hard—more like the shell of a nut—and inedible. This protects the sweet prize inside, the soft and fragrant juicy endocarp, which is segmented like a tiny white tangerine. But don't rush as you nibble on this ambrosial fruit: inside some of the pale syrupy segments is a dark pip about the size of a pumpkin seed.

Perhaps no other single fruit has been so widely coveted and for so long, than this, the "Queen of Fruits." European colonizers stumbled upon the mangosteen in Southeast Asia, and because the fruit spoiled so quickly, a rumor spread and became folklore that Queen Victoria herself would knight anyone who could bring her the fresh fruit.

The mangosteen is pricey, even by Hawaiian standards. At the fruit stand, we paid eighteen dollars for just five purple fruits. O but the taste is one for the poets—not unlike a creamy citrus, think a Creamsicle with a tartness of strawberries newly ripened under late May sunshine. Eric Mjöberg, a Swedish biologist, said, "It would be mere blasphemy to attempt to describe its wonderful taste, the very culmination of culinary art for any unspoilt palate."

European plant explorers in the late nineteenth century, such as F. W. Burbidge, Monsignor Jean-Baptiste Pallegoix, and Eric Mjöberg, wrote some of the earliest accounts of Europeans eating and enjoying the fresh mangosteen in its native environment. Burbidge had explored Borneo and described the flavor of the mangosteen as:

"Something like that of the finest nectarine, but with a dash of strawberry and pineapple added."

Pallegoix in Thailand also tried his hand describing the flavor:

"They exhume a sweet perfume approaching that of the raspberry and have the taste of strawberries."

Mjöberg went on to say this of the mangosteen:

"The mangosteen has only one fault; it is impossible to eat enough of it, but, strictly speaking, perhaps that is a defect in the eater rather than in the fruit."

Almost every description I've read and every local I talked to describes this fruit by naming another fruit, or a combo of fruits. *You're the poet,* one of my well-meaning friends says. *You come up with a description of how it tastes!*

Leave it to my pals to challenge me to do something that hasn't quite been accomplished in print since at least 1855. So here goes:

A mangosteen tastes like
Like   like   like—
like a poem with the word *ghost* in at least four different languages
a cage trap of lightning, a sheen of sugar in a bowl
like a memory of a plumeria tucked behind your Lola's ear
      when you crush a petal of mangosteen in your mouth,
        the juice runs clear

and smells the way certain plants sweeten their nectar at night
when they feel the tiptoe-crawl of a bee drawing near.
Crisp juice. Maybe more like a honeycreeper
buzzing your head
during golden hour. It's a bowl of chipped ice set out on a tray.
It's the wingbeat of a plover on the beach
of Hanalei.

SUGARCANE

So many cultures on this planet believe humans first sprouted from a stalk of sugarcane. Who is to say it isn't true? Aren't our hearts our blood our tendons and bones all sisters of sugar, all made of something meant to mumble in a mouth? Most sugar in the reed swells thickest just before the plant flowers. What does it mean to be cut down before so much sweetness?

Austronesian traders around 1200 to 1000 BC introduced sugar to India. Persians and Greeks encountered the famous reeds that produce "honey without bees" in India. By 400 BC, methods for manufacturing sugar from sugarcane had been developed in India. Only after the Crusades, when soldiers returned with what they perceived to be "sweet salt," did sugar begin to rival honey as the main sweetener in Europe.

When we moved to Mississippi, I discovered the Asian markets in Memphis carried barrels full of the purple stalks. My parents were visiting for the Christmas holidays at my request, because since they became grandparents I realized there's nothing material that I could ever want more than their presence for as many holidays as possible. I didn't get to see my grandparents very often, and I swore when I had kids they would get to know, really *know*, their grandparents.

Sugarcane is the world's most abundant crop. The most sugarcane ever cut by hand in eight hours is over 100,000 pounds, achieved in 1961 at a sugar farm in Australia. When sugarcane is harvested, it's cut just above the root level so new sprouts will grow, ready to be harvested again in ten to twelve months. The cane plants grow to be 10 to 20 feet high. An average sugarcane stalk weighs about 3 pounds but only has about .3 pounds of sugar. And a central narrative in Pacific mythologies places the sugarcane as no less than the origin for the human race—in the Solomon Islands they believed a single cane stalk brought forth a man and a woman, who thus became parents of the human race.

Diseases and worries for sugarcane farmers include: eyespot, mosaic, leaf scald, red rot, gumming disease, moth borers, leafhoppers, and grayback beetle larvae. Five U.S. states grow sugarcane: Florida, Louisiana, California, Hawaii, and Texas. Louisiana produced two million tons of sugar in 2022. In other words, the sugar produced by Louisiana's eleven sugar mills could fill up half the Superdome. Most of the American sugarcane crop is in Louisiana; with the exception of California, most sugarcane cannot grow very well north of Louisiana. The sugar crystallization process was first achieved by Étienne DeBoré at his plantation there.

The thick stalks of sugarcane contain a sweet juice, and that's what gets boiled down to make sugar. Any remaining liquid from the shredded stalks is also boiled down until it reduces to a thick liquid that becomes molasses. Blackstrap molasses is the most concentrated form and is particularly good for you, as it contains significant amounts of important nutrients like manganese, iron, and potassium.

Sugarcane is comprised of stalks, leaves, and a root system. Stalks can reach about thirty feet high and are broken up in segments called joints. At each joint, there is a node, where the long and thin leaves grow, fuzzy on the underside and smooth on the top. After emerging from the node, the leaves start to wrap themselves around the stems, and inside the stems are vascular bundles and the storage center for sugarcane juice. The sugarcane has a typical grasslike root system that is underneath the surface, but as the plant develops, it sends down anchor roots that can penetrate the earth from sixteen to twenty-two feet deep. Buttress roots support the plant and bring large quantities of water from a wide area.

While strolling the produce section at the Cordova International Farmer's Market with my parents, I picked up a stalk from the barrel and held it like a spear. *Sugarcane, Dad! Mom, don't you want sugarcane for Christmas Eve?* Both of their faces softened. My mom told me how she and my uncle used to buy sliced sugarcane for their walk to school each morning. My Lola Felipa would give her a few pesos for it. And she'd chew the pieces till all the cane juice was gone, as much as her little teeth could press. It's a story I've heard hundreds of times, but this time I noticed her face, smooth and wistful, as if she were looking far past the walls of the market, past the Mississippi River, the mountains, over the Pacific, and to her beloved islands. But then Dad interrupted her reverie and launched in with how he knows how to pick the ripest sugarcane, rummaging through the barrel and pulling up each one like purple lightsabers, because of course his daughter, not raised in a tropical zone, picked a not-so-sweet one. *Aha!* he exclaimed, holding one vertically, triumphantly, in each hand. *These are the best!*

And so that is how we ended up with two six-foot-tall stalks balanced between my two boys in our minivan on the hour-long drive home. That is how my dad ended up scrounging around all of the drawers in my kitchen, lamenting that we didn't have a big bolo knife, like they had in India and the Philippines. *No scythe in your home, Aimee! How do you live without one?*

Natives in Asia choose sugarcane as a treat. Sometimes mothers used it as a pacifier of sorts for babies, and children eat it mixed with rice. When Magellan arrived in the Philippines in 1521, natives in Mindanao offered sugarcane to his crew as a refreshment.

Over 75 percent of the world's sugar comes from sugarcane,

the rest from sugar beets. Part of the spread of sugarcane is a result of the method of cane propagation called *ratooning*—when the cane is harvested, a portion of the stalk buds are left underground on purpose so that more of the ratoon or stubble crop can grow again and again. The ratooning process can be economical, usually repeated three times, so that crops can be cultivated from one original planting. The yield of ratoon crops decreases after each cycle, and then all the stumps are plowed out and the field is replanted.

After Christmas Eve service, the glass bowl full of sugarcane slices my dad chilled for us was placed on the table on our back porch. We were still in church clothes. The boys, about eight and eleven at that time, had removed their bow ties and sat all boy-limbs over the armrests of the chairs, chomping away on the stalks like little ponies. Giggling at the burst of each first crunch and cronch, and O how I wish you could have seen their grandparents, eyes shining, watching them eat the same sweets from their own childhoods decades ago on the other side of this planet. We didn't have visions of sugarplums dancing in our head that night, but we had tropical fields swaying in the sea breeze. My parents cleared the way for us with a bolo knife. In so many varied ways. We danced to our sweet songs that night and woke to the boys squealing at what Santa had brought them. I can't remember a single present from that year. And I bet the boys can't either. But we remember the purple stalks. We remember the sugarcane, cut like celery sticks—the juice so cold and bright on our tongues.

FIGS

conjured up the courage to try figs again while I was teaching poetry for the summer on Thassos, a northern Greek island full of the most delicious blush-gold light, and salty breezes even on the hottest days in July. I wanted to get to the bottom of a fruity mystery from years ago, when a boy had told me the "crunch" of a fig meant I was eating a dead wasp. I had just plucked a fig from a fruit plate at one of our neighbor's parties and was happily crunching away as I surveyed the adults dancing. I don't even recall this kid's name, but he was a nephew or something of someone down the street. He showed up wearing red parachute pants and black-and-white-checkered sneakers and made quite the scene as he break-danced during dinner, or tried to, and was doing the robot and the worm, trying to get anyone to join him. I also remember the way he sidled up to me, watched me grab another fig, then sneered, "Aimee's eating bugs!" to the rest of the kids at the party. I tried to play it cool, but I put down the fig on my plate and was agog: *Could this jerk be right?!*

I'd believed this boy, and for thirty-plus years, the memory of what he said stayed with me, and I avoided the fruit. But they grow so easily in the sea air and soft Mediterranean light. After dinner in Greece, it was not uncommon to have fresh yogurt with a dollop of candied figs on top—spoon-sweets, the locals called them. I miss that simple sun-drenched bounty.

Figs are actually inside-out flowers—more like hundreds of flowers trapped inside a casing. The female fig wasp, still dusted with pollen from her own birth fig, enters an unripe fig through what is known as the ostiole, or the round base, stripping off her wings in the process. The wasp is so small, just two millimeters long—about the size of the tip of a crayon—and only lives for two days, during which she must safely penetrate the fig and lay her eggs among the tiny flowers, while also pollinating the flowers. She dies shortly after.

Male fig wasps emerge first from their galls—their egg casings—and, in a bit of seizure that I wish was still mysterious in my mind, tear a hole in the galls of the still-unhatched female larvae, fertilizing them even as they lay silent and growing. As the last act in their short lives, the males then dig a tunnel back out of the fruit before dying. When the females wake, they shimmy through these tunnels, catching pollen on their shiny new (fertilized) bodies, and then fly away, sometimes thirty miles above the canopy, where they search for the perfect unripe fig to lay their own eggs, continuing the cycle.

For more than nine thousand years, figs have been a keystone species, a critical component of the food web. Twelve hundred different kinds of animals depend on them, including a tenth of the world's birds, and, yes, the wasps who take their name from them. It's easy to imagine the rank appeal of taunting someone for gobbling up insect detritus. But if it seems like the boy who tried to gross me out all those years ago was right, you might be glad to know that the fruit's enzymes dissolve any remnants of wasps inside the fig. All that's left is the juice that Pliny the Elder called "the best food that can be taken by those who are brought low by long sickness."

I like to think of that first moment of crossing, when the female squeezes into the ostiole, shedding her wings. The wings, almost invisible, are left to scatter at the foot of the tree or nestle inside among the fig flowers. I like to think these wings are still able to flutter and fly and frolic in the form of a parrot or cuckoo or sweets-loving oriole. I don't worry the crunch; I celebrate the flight.

SHAVE ICE

Since most of my eighty-five-year-old mother's family mementos were destroyed during a typhoon in the Philippines, I've never seen any pictures of her as a child. But I imagine that I came close to seeing her childlike glee the day I treated her to Matsumoto's Shave Ice stand in Oahu.

We were visiting the famous North Shore during the holidays and couldn't pass up this shave ice institution, which has been serving the frozen concoction since 1951. The store itself is located in the historic town of Haleiwa, right off the main road. Its logo features a cup of shave ice with its rainbow spray of flavors striping a small mounded globe of ice. On a warm sunny day, the Matsumoto store serves over a thousand shave ices. When we were there in mid-December, there was a line out the door, and even weaving in and out of the key-chain racks, along the T-shirt displays, and looped around the aisles of snacks. As you get near the front, you can see the assembly line of shaves being made. With all the gorgeous colors, from lavenders to turquoise to chartreuse, I started to panic once I saw see the board full of flavors to choose from. I know friends that say you really can't go wrong, but I didn't want to be the first one to mess this up.

My boys and I tried their classic—rainbow: strawberry, lemon, and blue pineapple. I asked for an arc of mochi balls—each a little smaller than a ping-pong ball—arranged around the mound of ice. Though I'm sure others love it, I regretted the addition, as it turns out the shave ice didn't really need them; it was fruity and sweet aplenty. They also offered a drizzle of condensed milk, but again, the rainbow combo was so juicy on its own. Once we all got our orders, we sat at a picnic table and enjoyed a refreshing rest. Roosters pecked at the pebbles near our table; their iridescent feathers shone green and dark blue in that bright hour just before twilight. After a long day of walking around the North Shore, I think my parents were quietly glad to sit and rest. Their eyes shone with each bite of icy refreshment. My mom's beautiful cup looked like a scoop of frosted sunset—strawberry and mango, with a splash of liliko'i (passion fruit).

I was in Oahu to teach for the Iolani School in Honolulu. I taught and visited middle and high schoolers in the morning, and afternoons I spent with my whole family, visiting as much of the island as we could take in. None of us had been to Hawaii before, and I couldn't help but notice the large number of Filipinos all over the island, how comfortable my mom and I felt there, and how lovely it was to see Filipinos in advertisements and on billboards, and local people shopping with us in grocery stores and in the tourist traps.

Halfway during my visit, I put my hair down and clipped a plumeria barrette in my hair, and when I walked down the street a tourist asked *me* for directions. People thought I was from the island! At first I thought it was a fluke, but it became a running joke with my boys and Dustin giggling whenever I was stopped on the street as a local and asked questions—if I knew of a good restaurant nearby, if there was a place they could buy aspirin, and again if I could give directions. My boys have been present so many times when people back in the mainland would quip, *You speak English so well*, or when I've been asked the dreaded *What are you?* questions. Of course, I was fully aware that no matter what I looked like to the untrained eye, I was still a mainlander, but for a couple of weeks I got a taste of what it might be like, surrounded by people who look like me and my parents. Where I wasn't made to feel like an outsider for once.

I didn't realize how much history there was around ice's social function in Hawaii. In Hi'ilei Julia Kawehipuaakahaopulani

Hobart's brilliant book *Cooling the Tropics*, she chronicles how early on, in the mid-nineteenth century, freedom (especially for women and Indigenous peoples) was linked to the parlors that served ice cream and shave ice. As a result, warnings in magazines such as *Godey's Lady's Book* suggested that women who partook in iced beverages "were in great danger of incurable disease or even sudden death."

Restrictions followed, whether directly or indirectly official. *American Kitchen* magazine, shortly after the American annexation of Hawaii, printed, "a civilized being . . . can have oysters on the half shell brought in from Baltimore—to Neapolitan ice cream. . . . For the kanaka, there is abundant poi—poster paste five days old." In other words, the advertisements for cooled sweetness, an extravagance like ice cream, were targeted toward mainlanders—and in contrast, the native kanaka were encouraged to just be happy with room-temperature poi, even though they worked and farmed the land and would have almost certainly welcomed a frozen delight too.

It would be shave ice's lack of cream that would help it past these restrictions, as cream was the element that food "purists" who regulated native-owned and operated businesses could control. Shave ice would also prove an alternate take to the stereotypical tiki drinks that tourists made popular in the tropics and that were often a sign of colonialism.

You can find shave ice in many American cities as large as New York to as small as Oxford, Mississippi (although it is far too often incorrectly called *shaved ice*). The textures and tastes of fresh fruit found on the Hawaiian islands, like pineapples and lilik'oi, along with toppings like azuki beans and mochi make it identifiably different, as do the featherlike shavings that hold the tropical fruit syrup from pooling in the bottom of one's cup.

Favorite shave ice spots operate as a sort of inside scoop—

very much like the best crawfish spots or mudbug hookups in the American South. They trade on both insider knowledge and claims to authenticity. There are popular ones for the tourists, and ones where the majority of people waiting in line are natives. We also tried Waiola Shave Ice in Honolulu, a bit away from the glitzy designer stores on the main strip of Waikiki Beach. No neon sign, no sign really at all except a wooden painting of a scoop of rainbow shave ice. We tried the "Obama," with a joyous scoop of vanilla ice cream on the bottom and a striping of passion fruit, lime, and cherry syrups.

The next time I was in Hawaii, I was with girlfriends on the island of Kauai. On that island, we tried Jo Jo's and Wishing Well for shave ice because of the array of natural/organic flavors without the bright chemical coloring. I specifically chose my dear writer pals Beth and Sarah to accompany me at a friend's beach house, because I figured we could all use a break. All of us juggled COVID and writing and teaching and supervising our sons' online learning. All of us had leadership positions on our campuses, all of us active mentors of writers for years. All of us Asian American mothers and academics who have known all too well what it means and how often we have to put more effort into being heard. But shave ice was a reprieve from all of that. I wanted to give these friends the gift of just a couple of days of having their biggest stress be where and what to eat for dinner that someone else prepares for them. What toppings or fruit flavors to put in their cups of shave ice.

Beth had to leave a day early for a wedding on the West Coast, and on our last day, as we were driving back to the Lihue Airport, Sarah had a bright smile on her face and asked if we could go back to Wishing Well for one more shave ice. How could I refuse? Sarah, my friend for over twenty years, has a son the same age as my youngest, with the same fiery exuberance and temperament, so that when they are out in public together they are often mistaken for cousins. We packed up our bags, said goodbye one last time to the jewel-colored Hanalei Bay, and locked up the house.

No one asked us what we were as we stood outside Wishing Well, contemplating our last flavor combos. Sarah had liliko'i over macadamia nut ice cream and I had a fluorescent pink concoction of dragon fruit. We giggled over what we'd tell our families we did while we were away (sleep, read, dream, rest, eat, sing, laugh—literally zero debauchery) and thought, as we always do, of our mothers and younger sisters. And the twenty years of friendship and rooting for each other through breakups and marriage and kids and jobs and books. Our immigrant Filipina moms don't know each other, but I think they would be proud and amazed to know they raised girls who found a way to make a life in books and writing, and that their headstrong oldest girls found each other and are now giggling together over shave ice on an island in the North Pacific.

I'm so grateful for my women friends, who stay by my side when I'm down and when I'm up. Even as I write this, I can feel myself smiling, and isn't that what I tell my students? *If you can't feel it, we can't feel it:* what a gift, what a gift—thank goodness for friends. There was no set of directions anyone could have given me twenty-five years ago, when I was mostly broke and unpublished, that I would be able to follow correctly to get to that week on Kauai. Or that exact moment of elation and true peace I had in admiring the utter beauty and goodness radiated from Sarah's heart (and stomach!) as she scooped up each cool shiver of ice, sparkling in the morning sun like tiny comets in her spoon. A whole galaxy of gratitude.

BLACKBERRY

Gardening is an exercise in stubborn, fragrant faith: that these sticks that you hold in a feathery root ball will somehow turn pliant and shoot wild into the sunshine, offering fruit when you least expect it. But that's just what happened when my husband and I planted our first blackberry bush in late February on an unusually warm weekend here in Oxford, Mississippi.

For months, I was stubborn. I kept watering my sticks. Storms pounded our garden so hard that I thought for sure those sticks would wash away. But they held fast. And turned green and leafy. Then tiny white blossoms gave way to juicy whole blackberries by July. My youngest son, Jasper, gathered them in a blue bowl for his cereal in the morning. When the small harvests became less plentiful, Jasper suggested that maybe a fox or bear might have visited first—but his giggles (he couldn't even say it with a straight face) and his purpled chins and fingertips gave him away. By the hot-swell that first August, I was thinking of the Mary Oliver poem that ends with the line: "the black bells, the leaves; there is this happy tongue."

Children have few markers of time. My sons never wear watches, and neither have cell phones, but I love that they keep—as my youngest calls it—*fruit time*. May means strawberries, June is peaches, August equals watermelons, and September is persimmons. Now they have blackberries figured late into their summer and into their school year (here in the South, school starts early August). They know *blackberrying* as a verb. And since they were virtual learning that year—Zooming into their classes on a picnic table—one of their small joys was to get up between classes, wander over to the blackberry bush (which had grown taller now than either of them in just a few months), and pop a few sun-ripened drupelets into their mouths. A warm startle of juice edged the corners of their smiles when they weren't careful.

Since we were all outside so much during that time, we didn't need a scarecrow or whistle to shoo away the birds. It made me remember my youth—finding a blackberry patch with my neighbor when we were eleven, and oh, the *work* it took to gather a small cup full of them. But the sweetness was worth all the forearm scratches and pricks. We drew blood to gather blood-dark juice. Juice brilliant enough that people use it to dye cloth and hair. During the Civil War, blackberry tea helped alleviate dysentery, and sometimes temporary truces were called so Union and Confederate soldiers could pick blackberries together.

I still haven't completely processed all we lost during those years of the pandemic, how many funerals not attended, how many friendships strained under the weight of not seeing one another for years. I still haven't been able to pay my respects to my last grandparent who left this planet: my grandmother in India, who died peacefully in her sleep after a long, beautiful life. But blackberries gave us back a little bit of faith, gave us such bounty for our patience. When my sons gather the fruits, they share space with butterflies and birds and wasps in our yard, even a few skinks and anoles. These are also their classmates. They learn from them. And why not?

We shelter together in the cool shade, turn our faces to the sun, perk up when we hear a mockingbird, celebrate an evening rain shower. We close our laptops, put away our phones. We talk of getting another bush next year. Make plans to visit their grandparents again. I'm grateful to blackberries for helping my sons keep fruit time. No phones or clocks needed for this—this slowing down and taking notice. I'm certain this "happiness on our tongues" will last us *and* outlast us—the fruit that still grows (even though we've since moved across town) offers proof.

SABA BANANA

The first time I felt a quickening—the first kicks of my first pregnancy—the baby was about the size of a saba banana, heavier, but about the same length: four inches—in other words, just under the length of two baseballs. That's how I first pictured him, since Dustin played baseball in the local adult leagues and is an avid Cubs fan, so I had baseball on the brain. But no one tells you that really for each week you are pregnant, most measuring charts list an equivalent in the *produce* department and not in sporting goods: seven weeks, a blueberry; eleven weeks, a fig; nineteen weeks, a tomato; thirty weeks, a cabbage.

And since I was in the Philippines with Dustin and my mom, I decided I'd remember him and his fluttery kicks as a saba banana, one of the most important fruits in Philippine cuisine.

The saba banana is shorter than the typical banana here in the States, and has a squared-off shape, blocky even. The trees are about thirty feet tall with a dark, almost teal-blue trunk and leaves. I can't help but giggle at the hand imagery when talking about bananas. For instance, a bunch of saba bananas is sixteen hands, and each hand holds twelve to twenty fingers, or individual bananas. To this day, I can't even look at bananas in the store without thinking of them as *fingers*.

I'm convinced I had the quickening—this baby jumping—earlier than expected, because my baby was enjoying the delicious foods of his Lola's country: pancit, lumpia, duhat, mangoes, bangus, halo-halo on extra-hot days, rambutan already peeled for me by his father when I was just starting to waddle rather than walk. We were visiting my aunts and cousins in Bolinao during the New Year's holidays in 2006, and in the province's street fair that evening, the syrupy sweet smell of banana cue filled the air.

This street food is served on a bamboo skewer—sliced bits of saba banana dipped in light brown sugar and deep fried to a crackly perfection, with fluffy, piping hot, aromatic soft insides. Perfect for strolling (waddling) with your husband, watching the pickup basketball game of the locals wearing flip-flops but executing all manner of jump shots and spins, or looking up at some of the most spectacular and concentrated spills of stars you've ever seen.

You can eat saba bananas without cooking them, but they become more flavorful and tangy once cooked. They offer just about the same nutrition as potatoes, and you can boil or bake them, dice them into halo-halo, or crush them into banana ketchup—a favorite heady and sweet condiment around the world. They are some of the hardiest banana varieties on the planet, but farmers do have to worry over corm weevils and banana thrip infestations found in the fruit debris that gathers at the bottom of the trees.

And what of the invisible hands beckoning me to this place again? New Year's Eve festivities in the Philippines are a giant party like no other I've seen. All the islands seemed to be awake, eating, and karaoke machines in use all day long. A dog with three legs circled the block again and again till morning, a canine track star spooked by the lights and noise. Somewhere on the next block, a little girl was singing, "Hit me baby one more time . . ." trading places with her mom on karaoke for what seemed like an hour. The pop and fire of fireworks during daylight isn't unique to the Philippines for New Year's, but the feasting and gallivanting until the wee hours were a community joy I've not seen since.

Media Noche is the giant household meal at midnight, featuring twelve round fruits at the dinner table. At the exact stroke of midnight, children try to jump off furniture or jump as high as they can with coins in their pocket to grow taller and to be rich. It seemed like the whole province was in the streets, eating banana cue and strolling, strolling. The crowd in the town square started swelling, so we headed inside as it grew closer to midnight. I didn't want to be around loud firecrackers for the baby in my belly's sake. I told my husband to jump for all three of us. But what I remember was his hands—

His hands holding mine, then moving to my belly to see if he could catch a flutter or kick or small punch of our boy, who was a saba banana that week. As tall as an apple the week before. We noticed the baby was a wee bit nocturnal, but we could never fully predict when he'd start dancing. After Media Noche, I was nibbling small bites of leche flan for dessert, and sure enough— soon you could see the baby's knee or elbow swipe across the skin of my belly, as if he were trying to wipe a fogged mirror with his hands, but the mirror was my belly, and he was trying to get a better view of us. Or maybe he was simply signaling he wanted more dessert, *more, more!*

Dustin and I were on the couch by then, and my cousins and mom were getting ready to retire for the evening. Dustin put his hands on my tummy, and I set my plate down and put my hands over his hands. That night might have been the first time we were feeling one another's hands, the *three* of us, I mean, fingers spread wide to fit over my widened belly. I had no idea how much my hands would or could hold. I learned that a mama's hands could hold much more than she ever dreamed she could want to. It seemed utterly impossible then that in just five more months, our baby would grip my pinky in the center of *his* whole hand, but it happened, again and again (how I loved it especially when he was soporific from nursing!), and now as I type this, his hands are *bigger* than mine and they don't reach for mine as often these days, but some days they do, still, when no one is looking, and I can't think on it too much or I'd weep. But back then, under thousands of stars—all six of our hands stretched wide and ready to catch a bounty of squeals, cries, and laughter headed toward us in the new year.

STRAWBERRY

When I was little, one of the most popular toys in America smelled like strawberries. Or more specifically, it was a sweet-syrupy plastic cake smell. Strawberry Shortcake wore an oversize pink-and-white polka-dotted bonnet, with green-and-white-striped tights, and her hair was a marvelous confection of deep-red gloss, pressed. It looked like candy floss. I shudder to think what chemicals the kids of the 1970s and '80s were huffing regularly: colored markers, scratch n' sniff stickers, and the whole village of Berry Patch dolls. Strawberry Shortcake was the main character; Mr. Sun and other Berry Patch pals all had adventures with her and went about their day watching over and tending their gardens—except when the villain of Berrytown, known as the Baker of Porcupine Peak, lurched and danced his way over to Berrytown and stole all the berries for his pies.

~

Strawberries are members of the rose family. Their botanical name is *fragaria*, which means fragrance. The first syllable of its common name seems to come from the word *strew*, a nod toward how the runners (the horizontal stems that advance along the ground) spread this fruit so easily that the fruit seems to be strewn on the ground.

~

The Strawberry Shortcake doll resembles a stuffed rag doll come to life, with a sprinkle of distinctive freckles. A blunt red fringe on her forehead peeks out of her floppy bonnet. I was obsessed with the fact that she lived in a house made of shortcake with her sassy cat, Custard. My mother never let me have one of those dolls from the world of Strawberry Shortcake, though she gave me a doll named Sindy instead, which was supposed to be *cherry*-scented. Sindy was not shaped like a girl, but a full-on curvaceous woman. Think Barbie, but with electric-red hair that smelled like synthetic cinnamon and grape cough medicine. As she presented it to me one day after work, my mother said, "Look! See here is a doll that smells like cherries! Go ahead, take this!" But I knew cherries from our Fourth of July celebrations, and this pungent, oily chemical concoction . . . was not it. I was the kind of girl who loved tiny Matchbox cars instead, and if my memory serves, I think I cut off Sindy's hair, since that is where the rich odor seemed to come from. My mother was not pleased—one, that her eldest seemed to prefer cars over dolls, save for the one from Berrytown, and two, she kept finding sprinkles of electric-red hair on the floor, no matter how much she vacuumed.

~

When my husband and I were writing our wedding invitations, to delineate the date, we asked the stationer to inscribe *on the cusp of berry season*, as in, *May 29, on the cusp of berry season*. But all our friends knew that since we were married at the end of May in western New York, I really meant *strawberry* season. For my money, that's the best berry season of the whole summer—one of the first fruits to ripen fully in late spring.

~

Ancient records reveal that Rome had strawberries all the way back to 200 BC. Romans used strawberries to treat depression, fever, and sore throats. The Greeks, however, had an aversion to any type of red fruit, believing it was poisonous or filled with mysterious powers. If you were with child, you were told to avoid them so that you wouldn't give birth to a baby with strawberry-shaped splotches on their body.

~

The ground is usually wet and chilly in those late spring days, even if the heat and humidity of summer approaches with something like a soft sigh in your ear during the day. But before the swelter comes the strawberry—its dainty white flowers promise summer is near. The strawberry was a symbol for Aphrodite, the goddess of love, because of its heart shape and red color. Its flowers remind me of Bella, our cherubic blond flower girl that year (who I'm delighted to report has just graduated college!), who wore a white dress with flower petals sewn in the top layer and a crown of white flowers in her hair. I can see it so clearly now—she was a walking strawberry flower to herald me down the aisle to my Love.

~

The allure of the strawberry was particularly strong in Europe. Madame Talian, a common fixture in the court of Emperor Napoleon, became famous for filling a tub with the juice of fresh strawberries for a distinctive and unusual bath. For this berry special dip, it was estimated she had servants gather twenty-two pounds per basin. Needless to say, this was not a daily occurrence. In its heyday, the garden of Charles V of France boasted twelve hundred strawberry plants—a magnificent number to be planted in any one place in Europe. Even today, one of the most popular exhibits at Belgium's Strawberry Museum, or the Musée de la Fraise, is the Jardin des Petits Fruits—a berry garden filled with fresh tiny temptations in the summer. The dessert of strawberries and cream was made famous by Thomas Wolsey in King Henry VIII's court, and his second wife, Queen Anne Boleyn, had a strawberry-shaped birthmark on her neck. Several court advisers claimed this mark was proof of her being a witch, and cited that as yet one more reason for her to be beheaded. On the menu at the annual Wimbledon tennis tournament is strawberries and cream, one of the most popular dessert combos and something of a tradition to consume while watching an exciting match, often with British royalty peppering the stands.

~

In 1843, growers in Cincinnati were the first to be able to ship chilled strawberries by placing blocks of ice on top of boxes containing the berries, forever making strawberries able to last longer—more time to savor that sweetness. Strawberries are famous for being able to spread and cover a corner or patch in your garden quickly, but they don't usually grow from seed. Instead, strawberry plants send out runners, which grow very close to the surface of the soil and stretch horizontally. The roots then produce new plants that are often used as starts to share with others.

~

Vikings believed that when a baby died they ascended to the heavens in the form of a strawberry—the seeds of strawberries represented the souls of babies. For the Vikings, eating a strawberry was akin to eating a baby. Very frowned upon, to say the least.

~

I'm always startled by the folks pranking others by taking pictures of various white animals (mostly bunnies, rats, white monkeys, and cats with white fur) who seem calm but for the blaze and flash of a juicy-red and messy mouth. It looks like they just took a bite of a fresh heart, or raw meat, and of course, the reveal is not that a bunny turned out to be a *carnivore*, but rather that they were simply fed strawberries.

~

During the pandemic I followed a Japanese woman who lived by herself with five teacup Chihuahuas. They seemed isolated, and at least in her postings, it didn't seem like she had much connection or interaction with anybody, even from a distance. She often gave the Chihuahuas a type of biscuit while she made Japanese sponge cakes, and perhaps the main reason why I followed her is that these cakes were mesmerizing—formed with soft, precisely cut sweetbread, then rolled with whipped cream and perfectly diced fruits, mostly strawberries. I became used to these soothing daily posts, but the description was all in Japanese.

The eldest Chihuahua died just a few months into the pandemic, and I couldn't look away from how she continued to dress up this little dead dog and place it in a basket in her apartment courtyard. Her other four dogs ran around the basket, full of dead dog. She even picnicked with all of them and continued to make her sponge fruit sandwiches. But after this went on for days, and no sign of finally saying goodbye or burial or getting rid of the dead Chihuahua (who was still wearing baby clothes), I unfollowed her. It was all too much for my heart, and I felt so sorry for this lady on the other side of the planet munching on her perfectly sliced strawberry sandwiches, and I can't actually remember her name or how to even look it up because it was all in Japanese characters. I don't even know how to search for her again. I hope and wonder if she is okay.

~

When you slice the strawberry vertically it looks like a cartoon heart. I never knew until the nineties, when my friends started to get married, that you can cut strawberries into even more delicate shapes, such as double roses and swans, and that they'd still hold their shape at least through a wedding reception. I never knew you can make "Strawberry Wine," until it became Song of the Year by Deana Carter—a slow summer love song that stayed on the Billboard charts for twenty weeks during my last year of college, when I was preparing to say goodbye to my college boyfriend, who was off to law school in another city.

~

Growing up on the grounds of a mental hospital made day trips with my family off the grounds extra special. When my mom had weekends off, my dad would announce that we'd be exploring these back roads of western New York. On one of these trips, we saw a sign that said YOU PICK crudely painted on a slab of wood, and I imagine it was hard for my parents to pass up that sweetness, especially for my mom, after a long week of intense work with her patients. At the farm stand, we were each given a green cardboard pint container, and the lady at the fruit stand simply said *Have fun.*

~

O the berries turned into sugar quickly underneath the late spring sunshine of western New York. O I never understood the need for sugar at thirteen, never even had the taste for it until strawberry season came around. The berries at this You Pick farm were just bigger than a golf ball, the size of two if you got there early enough in the season, and the berry patches stretched out and out and extended to the horizon, as far as my eye could see. We were still fairly new to that sleepy little town—one of the only Asian American families in the village of Gowanda. I never understood how, after living for years in Arizona suburbs surrounded by sparsely planted cacti, my dad knew how to find all the best berry patches in a two-hour radius, semi-hidden in all this new green and green and green of deciduous trees in late May and early June. But before we started our new school, he helped us get to know this new green spot we'd call home for the next four years. And before the first day of classes, he taught us how to tell time by what fruit was in season each month. May and June: strawberries. July: cherries. August: blueberries. And it was the strawberry we all learned to reach for first.

~

Fast-forward twenty-six years later: I have an almost-three-year-old kicking and giggling in a car seat behind me and a six-year-old next to him in his car seat. A job brought me back to western New York at a small college in the area, and I find the berry patch sign from my favorite place to pick strawberries. The sign has been painted over and redone now, but I'd recognize it anywhere. We were supposed to get groceries, maybe stop at the bookstore, but that sign drew me in again. I couldn't pass it up. I wanted to be there when my boys first grab the berries from my hand and nibble on them with such abandonment, such a love and hunger and thirst that their mouths end up looking like those goofy bloody bunny pictures. I wanted to be there to guide their hand, to guide their feet on the straw-lined walkways to keep them from stepping on the fruit and teaching them how to squat and look under the leaves for that surprise of red. I wanted to remember the exact shade of red when summer bursts with sugar and berry light.

VANILLA

When I think of vanilla, I think of boys. My son is in high school now and knows how to scrape a vanilla bean, starting from the center, cutting a slit with the tip of a sharp knife. He knows how to spread the bean apart to expose the seeds and scratch with the dull side of the knife. He knows how to slide the sticky seeds off the side of the knife. I don't think he remembers us actually making vanilla extract together, but we have pictures taken by Dustin to prove it.

We wouldn't even have vanilla ice cream, vanilla perfumes, vanilla flavors and desserts without a boy—specifically a twelve-year-old enslaved child named Edmond Albius. Edmond's mother died when he was a baby on the island of Réunion, off the coast of Madagascar, and the man who enslaved Edmond was a botanist who fussed and fumed over his vanilla orchids, which simply would not bloom. In 1836, a Belgian scientist observed the Melipona bee—native only to Mexico—pollinating vanilla flowers, something that had posed a problem for plantation owners in the tropics who also wanted to grow this expensive spice, the most expensive spice on the planet, second only to saffron. Historians don't know if Edmond was ordered to find a solution or if he came up with it on his own, but in 1841 Edmond developed by trial and error the technique that is still used today all over the world to pollinate vanilla orchids.

Vanilla vines grow about thirty to fifty feet tall, but farmers found when you bend them and keep them low they produce more flowers. These flowers on the vine survive in hot and humid climates only a few hours, making hand-pollination extra difficult, because they open in the morning and shrivel up by noon in the hot sun. Vanilla orchids smell sweet and slightly smoky, like cinnamon. And they contain both female and male parts in one flower. I adore this noticing, this careful observation of an enslaved child—that he was looking so carefully at flowers, these pale-greenish white flowers with yellow hairs on the lip giving off a cylindrical bloom—how closely he must have examined them to come up with his idea when no one else on the planet had before him. Edmond used a shard of bamboo to lift up the thin membrane, the rostellum, that separated the anther sac and the stigma of the orchid blossom so that they touched, but to give them a little extra connection Edmond smooshed them together with his finger and thumb. If pollination, or as botanists call it, marriage, works, the thick green base of the flower swells almost immediately and eventually into a fingerlike seed pod that ripens yellow, then brown. About nine months later, just like the gestation period of a human baby, the vanilla beans are ready to be harvested, making this the only edible fruit of the orchid family.

When vanilla beans finish drying in the sun during the day, a flavor and fragrance profile containing over five hundred organic compounds emerges. When the pod shrivels and becomes supple, they turn a dark brown color and then give off a noticeable vanilla aroma. You should be able to wind and tie a bean around your finger and be able to untie it again without it breaking—that's how flexible it should be.

Other white botanists of course tried to claim it was their idea, but in a rare form of solidarity and justice, Albius's enslaver actively defended his discovery and invited other plantation owners to see what Edmond had discovered. In fact, the owner wrote letters to publishers and editors to guarantee that Albius was included in the island's historical encyclopedia, even when other botanists tried to take credit. In his letter to the official historian of the island of Réunion, Edmond's enslaver wrote, "I have been [Richard's] friend for many years, and regret anything which causes him pain, but I also have my obligations to Edmond. Through old age, faulty memory, or some other cause, M. Richard now imagines that he himself discovered the secret of how to pollinate vanilla, and imagines that he taught the technique to the person who discovered it! Let us leave him to his fantasies."

I think of Edmond Albius and the unwritten history of how his enslaver noticed his noticing of plants, allowing Edmond to study plants alongside him instead of doing hard labor like the rest of the plantation's enslaved population. And of all of Edmond's hours spent among vanilla orchids, pressing his face close to the blooms, marrying flowers to make fruit when there was no record of him fathering any children of his own, even after he was granted his freedom. I won't pretend to think the scent of vanilla calmed his heart while he wasn't free, but his story is one of the rare moments of at least approaching some small bit of validation—when a white man gave him entire (not even partial) credit for developing a whole branch of industry, even when another white botanist insisted Edmond copied his original technique.

A hybrid variety of orchid *Vanilla tahitensis* created in the Philippines was brought to French Polynesia and grown on small plantations largely by families of Chinese immigrants. These beans are shorter and plumper than other vanilla beans, and their smell is distinctly floral and highly prized by pastry chefs. Because of our Filipino heritage, this is the kind of vanilla bean I specifically wanted to use for the first homemade gifts Pascal, my eldest son, and I made back when he was in kindergarten and we still lived in western New York. Vanilla extract is the cutest homemade gift to make with kids—all you need to have are two ingredients, vanilla beans and alcohol.

Big lake-effect snowstorms were predicted, so we prepared for a weekend indoors by the fireplace. A few weeks earlier I had ordered Tahitian vanilla beans and bought little amber apothecary jars, about four ounces apiece. Tahitian vanilla beans are floral and fruity, with a cherry-like flavor.

To make gift bottles of vanilla extract, I printed out sticker labels for the bottles that said it was ready to use in about three months. Because Pascal was still learning to cut paper in a straight line and in smooth curves, I carefully slit open the vanilla beans lengthwise to expose the seeds. Those days I would draw long swoops of lines in marker on colorful pieces of construction paper to help him practice cutting smooth, oh my heart to think of those sweet long days of me reading next to him while he practiced cutting paper, some lite yacht rock songs probably playing in the background, and now—*poof!*—we are looking at colleges together.

For a 4-ounce (1/2 cup) small bottle: You will need 2 beans and 1/2 cup of any plain vodka. I had Pascal carefully cut the beans in half to help them fit in the bottles more easily. We used Grade B beans, which are drier and not as supple, but the flavor itself is much more concentrated and ideal for vanilla extract, even if the beans are a bit more physically blemished and jagged compared to the glamorous Type A beans. Just make sure the beans are covered in vodka, and tighten the lid and shake it just a little bit.

Pascal loved this part, and I had to ask him to be gentle, as he wanted to shake all the finished bottles as if he were holding a pair of maracas in each hand. If you use amber glass like we did, you can keep it on your kitchen counter, but if you use clear glass, you need to keep it in a dark cupboard or pantry, else it will evaporate and/or turn cloudy when exposed to sunlight. I printed a note with each jar saying to leave the seeds in the bottle, because then you can add more vodka when it gets low and let it sit for three months again, as the beans are potent enough to last for at least two batches of vanilla extract.

In the fourteenth century, the Yuan dynasty invented ice cream, which was served at court. In the eighteenth century, the French started adding vanilla to ice cream. The Marquis de Sade requested vanilla pastilles sent to him while in jail. Madame Pompadour, mistress of King Louis XV, liked to have vanilla chocolate flavored with ambergris accompanied by celery soup and a handful of truffles at dinner. Vanilla itself was introduced to the United States through France, even though Mexico already grew it back when Thomas Jefferson requested that a friend in Paris ship him fifty batons wrapped in newspapers. Jefferson's original recipe for ice cream called for a stick of vanilla, and he's credited as the first American to write down an ice cream recipe. Hundreds of years later, vanilla is often added to other ice cream flavors, as it helps to enhance and augment their taste. It's now the most consumed flavor of ice cream in the world.

But because the production of vanilla is so costly, scientists have experimented with creating vanilla substitutes. One of these substitutes is castoreum—a secretion from the anal glands and castor sacs of beavers, that use it to stake their claims and spray their dams in a pond, marking territory. Castoreum extract possesses a warm, sweet odor and may be used as a stand-in for vanilla extract in many dairy products and baked goods. It is interesting to note, though, that because castoreum is extracted from an animal source, it is considered a natural flavor, so that is something to ponder when you read a list of ingredients of a processed food that has a vanilla aroma or flavor in it, for my vegan friends especially.

Even with that knowledge, vanilla was recently named the world's favorite smell. Scientists from the University of Oxford and the Karolinska Institutet in Stockholm presented 10 scents to 235 people from 9 different cultures around the world, and selected people from urban areas in the United States and Mexico;

hunter-gatherer groups from the Southeast Asian rainforest (such as the Semaq Beri people from the Malay Peninsula in Thailand); fishing communities from Central America's Pacific coast; as well as secluded farmers living in the South American mountains, as their sample sniffers. All agreed on the scent of fresh vanilla as their favorite.

In real estate markets in the United States, vanilla is the main scent realtors suggest for open houses and potential buyer visits: put a drop of vanilla on a cookie sheet and turn on the oven for about fifteen minutes, then turn it off again to give that "freshly baked cookies smell." Aromatherapists say the smell of vanilla can create feelings of comfort, peace, and contentment.

I think back to when I first made vanilla with my eldest. I remember that storm blew in almost two feet of snow that weekend, more than waist-high on my five-year-old. We were farther from a tropical island than we ever had been. Our pipes were surely in danger of freezing. But that weekend, my son sat smooshed up alongside me on the couch as we used a coffee table for our homemade lab-kitchen. The first gift we made together—little bottles of vanilla extract for our loved ones. Outside they closed the Thruway. No one was allowed to drive unless it was an emergency. Inside a little ranch house, a mother was teaching her son how to tie a bow of red-and-white baker's twine for each gift tag. How to make something that wouldn't stay yours, but would be a remembrance of the grace in slowing down and thinking of the future, of others' happiness. That weekend indoors with my family, no matter how much we washed, our fingertips stayed oiled with the scent of vanilla beans and the tiniest whiff of orchids for days.

KAONG

Elephant ear plants—as big as a car door—press to the ground. Press, shimmy, and press again to the ground as they wait for afternoon rains. Press, shimmy, press. I'm here in Singapore as a visiting poet for a local university, and I've brought my mother along so she could see the famed botanical gardens and cloud forest.

One of the trees we saw in abundance there was the sugar palm tree, known for many as the Tree of Hope; not only can you make so many products from it—furniture, baskets, wood floors, flour, and even bread from the inner pith—but for riparian communities in Asia, sugar palm trees are vital. At about sixty-five feet tall, sugar palms are a huge slope stabilizer for riverbanks during heavy rains and wind, and they help prevent precious soil from being washed away thanks to their fingerlike roots holding fast and steady in a storm.

The fruit of the sugar palm is called kaong, a treasure of Filipino fruit salads and one of my favorite ingredients in halo-halo. Encased in a green baseball-size seed covering are three or four kaong fruits. You can eat them raw, but I love them boiled in a sugar syrup, glazed and glistening like polished pieces of milky quartz. When I eat halo-halo, I save each translucent paper-clip–size piece for last because I love their sticky, chewy texture, especially when they are chilled from being surrounded by powdered ice.

On one of my off days, we dined at Plaza Singapura, a giant mall set right in the jeweled heart of the shopping district. At lunchtime, a little girl of about five or six, with jet-black bangs cut straight across her eyebrows, ran away from her own birthday party and into the mall. We were more than halfway through our meal when she came running back, breathless, clearly lost and looking for her parents. She ran right to our table and asked me how to get back to her party. While I walked her around the restaurant, looking for a manager, she told me unbidden and matter-of-factly that she had no favorite color. None at all. I'd never heard such a thing—not having a favorite color, especially for a child! In giant ceramic containers, aranda orchids held up five petals in a tired wave at us.

Turns out, after walking all over the mall—past the perfume counters and the free hand massage stations and the tea shops—the little girl's birthday party was just in the back corner of our same restaurant. Even though their kid was missing for almost half an hour, the parents didn't say thank you. Even frowned a bit when I brought her back to them.

After a gorgeous and humid morning at the orchid gardens, my mother and I were planning to have halo-halo for dessert before this drama of the missing birthday girl, and well—what's better after a long day in the stickiness of the outdoors than ice-cold kaong sinking in halo-halo ice? Halo-halo is surely the coldest thing in this whole country—cold as a toucan would be in the arctic with a mouth full of guava. Now watch it chip and chip its fruit-beak into the side of an iceberg, freshly calved. What falls into the sea, scooped up and sugared with cream, is almost like the first bite of halo-halo. Almost. You have to try it yourself to see.

Maybe the girl who had no favorite color will grow to love the almost colorless kaong in a bowl of halo-halo, too—and maybe years later, when someone asks her about her favorite color, say, as she rides a bus on her way to school, and she'd rather look out the window—maybe she will finally answer: *the color of kaong*. *Kaong*, she will say. *My favorite color is kaong*.

WATERMELON

'm pretty sure it was a Caveman who gave me my first slice of the iciest sugar-sweet watermelon I've ever had in my entire life. That's what the members of the football team of Cave City, Arkansas, are called—there's a sign in town that says HOME OF THE CAVEMEN. Ross agreed to meet up in Memphis on one of the darkest, stormiest weekends of the summer to make our way over to the Cave City Watermelon Festival to check out the "World's Sweetest Watermelons." The sky was in peak darkness during a new moon—the thunder moon, or halfway summer moon, had just turned black. Meanwhile, an old Balkan folktale says that a full moon can turn a field of watermelons into vampires, but lucky for us, the night sky that weekend was rendered in utter darkness, a new moon.

For over five thousand years people have noshed on watermelons. It originated in Sudan, where early watermelons had white flesh not nearly as sweet as the ones we've come to know and love since then. Mark Twain famously adored watermelon, calling it "king by grace of God over all the fruits of the earth. When one has tasted it," he continued, "he knows what the angels eat."

The whole state seemed excited about this festival, especially after a few years of quiet—the festival was canceled first due to the pandemic, and then the next year due to heavy rains, which turned the vines too gooey to produce good fruit. The festival, a celebration of the sweetest watermelons in the United States, is just a few hours away from where I live in Mississippi, and I couldn't resist the thought of meeting Ross there after our own pandemic years apart. At the very least, I couldn't imagine another writer pal who would be as keyed up about watermelons as I was, and also, as a former college football lineman, he made a great companion through the isolated highways winding around the Ozarks. Our plan was to consume a mountain of melons, tasting all the varieties we could find—like Orange Krush, or maybe some Sentinels—and seeing if they were indeed the best.

It thundered and stormed at our reunion, and I started looking up directions to various watermelon farms around the area, assuming the festival was surely going to be kaput. But finally we got word that the festival was still on, except for the races and watermelon games, canceled because of the giant puddles in the fields, but that didn't deter us, and we headed out. There was a chill in the air when we arrived, and I kicked myself for not bringing a hoodie—the very thing I always remind my children to pack *just in case*. I figured it was just going to be a few days, and it was the end of July, so I only thought to pack sundresses as if it was going to stay in the nineties, like usual that time of year.

Besides the canceled 5K melon dash and throwing games, the festival promised us a pancake breakfast, a watermelon parade, and cloggers, and then of course the thing we were most excited about: the free watermelon feast. (I still couldn't figure out how it would be *free*. Surely they'd ask for a donation?) Before that, Ross was intent on finding fried dough—his one junk-food indulgence that I know of—and I wandered over to the craft section, looking for pretty soaps, but got sidetracked by a man selling birdhouses.

This was the first festival I'd been to since COVID started, and so stopping at each table to visit with the seller for a bit seemed like such a glorious luxury. I often travel alone, and because of some pretty scary experiences with strangers, I don't open up to new people as much as I'd like to. But knowing that Ross was nearby, chatting up another booth or checking on his fried dough truck, made me perfectly relaxed, and I met a whole community of people selling bandannas for dogs, various trivets, and wooden signs burned with the words LIVE, LAUGH, LOVE on them. A farmer

I spoke to said that to grow a sweet and healthy watermelon, you need four things: water, sun, bees, and a well-drained sandy soil. It's the soil within a fifteen-to-twenty-mile radius of Cave City that makes the watermelons so sweet and gives them their unique flavor, he explained.

The fried dough truck never seemed to open, much to Ross's chagrin. But we overheard some volunteers murmuring, *The feast, the feast, the feast!* It was as though we were all invited to a secret Midsummer party. Soon, some strapping teens—the (mostly white) high school football team, aka the Cavemen—pulled up a giant freezer truck into the back of the park and started passing out watermelons like a bucket brigade down onto some folding tables where other Cavemen and Cavemen dads were ready with large knives for slicing.

This event, held just behind the Melon Stage, was the festival's pièce de résistance, talked up the previous day by locals at the various farm stands and grocery stores with big smiles and shimmery eyes, all saying it was the bee's knees and not to miss it. There were so many people crowding around the freezer truck, and even though there were not nearly as many black and brown folks present as I might've hoped, I was happy to see at least some gathered nearby, especially since the festival website and promotional flyers advertised only white people in attendance.

The line started to snake through the park paths and back up to the refrigerated truck. I worried everyone would get only a tiny wedge, maybe a thin circle slice if we were lucky. Then I noticed one of the Cavemen dads slicing the elongated melons not crosswise, like you would for pickle chips, but lengthwise, like you would for pickle spears. Every single one of us was handed a giant horizontal wedge of watermelon the size of a loaf of bread. When I looked up, I saw hundreds of people facedown in watermelon—giggle-dribble-laugh-spitting seeds. It was magnificent—there's really no other word—to see people of all sizes, ages, shapes, and color hauling their giant slices with both hands to their own corner of the park to nibble down with their loved ones.

Ross got his slice and moved over to a tree to gobble it up, and I started on mine. The flesh was so *cold*, I swear I could taste the crystalline sugar granules in each icy bite. One lady who worked at the festival selling T-shirts told me that the freezer truck was turned up as high as it could go without freezing the melons solid. A cool breeze tickled my wet chin and cheeks. We were all drooling pink juice, and I didn't even realize it until a sweet girl (possibly a Cavesister?) began passing out paper towels to everyone. Combined with the still-wet fields and rain puddles from earlier that day, we were, as they say, a hot mess trying to eat this fruit, which is over 90 percent water. (It's no surprise that travelers crossing the Kalahari would once hollow out the sturdy exteriors, fill them with water, and carry them as canteens on their journeys.)

Every person around me held a slice chin-level as they ate, giant cartoon smiles where their small mouths should be. I can't remember if Ross and I even talked to each other while we ate. I think we didn't. I for one was astonished and in disbelief at this sweetness in the here and now. I looked over at Ross and it was hard not to smile at my dear friend enjoying his slice, concentrating and furrowing his brow once in a while, thinking hard. He is one of those rare friends whom you can be quiet with. We could just be loud and nearly crying with laughter one minute, then completely silent the next.

I found out later that one of the most abundant melons at this year's festival was indeed the variety called Orange Krush. The color of its flesh is a pale butterscotch candy or a light amber. At the feast I had one slice of that and one of the reds—probably the 720 or perhaps a Royal Sweet. There are about seven local families who all grow melons for this festival, many of them on their fourth generation of farmers, and in order to be deemed an official grower and get the special white oval Cave City Watermelon sticker, you must register with the Cave City Chamber of Commerce. Like Georgia's Vidalia onion, only melons grown in the Cave City area of Sharp County can bear the name Cave City Watermelon. Even if I grew melons here in Mississippi with seeds from Cave City watermelons, they wouldn't be Cave City melons.

An older lady wearing a watermelon-printed visor walked around the park saying, *Rinds in the truck! Throw the rinds in the truck!* And though neither of us saw it pull up, sure enough an old blue Chevy with a giant empty flatbed had appeared. When everyone finished chowing down on their melon slice, they threw the rinds into the truck bed, where they'd land with a juicy splash, possibly to be fed to pigs and horses afterward, Ross guessed.

When I teach poetry in Northern Greece during the summer, a common wake-up call is the sound of the local farmers driving their flatbeds full of watermelon as they wind their way around the island countryside of Thassos, calling out *Karpouzi! Karpouzi! Karpouzi!* It's one of my favorite terms of endearments for my sons, even if all traces of their little Karpouzi bellies have vanished over the years. In Japan, you can find cubed watermelons, a little bigger than a Rubik's cube, cultivated inside plastic frames, boutique geometric varieties that often sell for a hundred dollars. So different than the small, dusty cannonballs on Thassos.

Most people knock to test whether watermelons are ripe. You should hear a soft hollow thump, not a metallic ringing, which would mean it's still not ready to eat. If you're at a farm, you can also inspect the tendrils or the pigtails of the vine—if they've turned brown near the melon, it's ripe for picking. You'll want to cut it from the vine instead of yanking or twisting it off, which could allow a bacteria or fungus into the flesh and turn it sour.

The side of the melon lying against the ground should produce a little ground spot that turns a buttery yellow. And of course, the heavier the better.

The heaviest watermelon on record was grown by Chris Kent of Sevierville, Tennessee, verified by the Great Pumpkin Commonwealth in 2013, and weighed just over 350 pounds, about as much as an upright piano. The Cave City Watermelons weren't nearly that heavy—I could carry them without much trouble. As we headed out of town, we stopped at the first roadside stand to bring some back for our beloveds. We checked the melons to make sure they had the official Cave City Watermelon sticker on them, and picked up about five or so *each* to load up into Ross's rental car. Once you harvest them, the farmer said, they're good for two to three weeks, but best and crispiest within the week.

We left Arkansas early the next morning, sated. Driving in that wide-open space between Memphis and rural Arkansas, we passed fields and fields of something planted in neat rows. It was not an accidental prairie or meadow, but seemed to be a purposeful arrangement of some kind of fruit with dots of red inside, something neither of us had ever seen. We pulled over to get a better look. We walked up the gravelly edge of the driveway—was it a farm?—to one of the rows of plants, and we saw that it wasn't fruit at all. We must have had fruit on the mind, I guess, because what we thought was a fruit or vegetable was actually a beautiful flower—a bright pinkish-red flower.

We hadn't seen a car for miles, and suddenly I realized we were very much alone. I don't know if Ross noted that, too, or if that is something that, as a woman, I'm used to worrying over. We were standing in this field, nothing but a barn and a seemingly empty farmhouse for miles, and Ross and I squatted, smelling and rubbing the waxy leaves. I looked it up on one of my plant apps on my phone and learned that it was a member of the *Gos-*

sypium family. I couldn't believe it, but sure enough—we were in a field of cotton. There we were, two brown people *oohing* and *aahing* over cotton! Ross doesn't scare easily, but it didn't take much to sense that neither of us felt right out there in a field of cotton in the South. We both hustled back to the rental car pretty quickly without saying a word.

With Ross behind the wheel, we wound our way back to Memphis, where I'd left my car, and he'd continue to head east from there to see his mom on his birthday. As we drove past more cotton fields in full bloom, I kept thinking back to an event we once had done together. This was in Florida, years earlier, before any of our prose books had come out, when we were still known as poets, *just poets*. I remember asking him that night, *What if this is the last time we're ever onstage together?* Ross just grunted, looked up at the stars, and shook his head in disbelief. *If we don't do any more readings together, that means*—he paused—*we're dead!* And what do you say to *that* affirmation, morbidly funny though it may be? He's right, of course, but hopefully not for a long, long, *long* time.

Ross and I spent a weekend surrounded by hundreds and hundreds of watermelon slices. I ate more watermelon in forty-eight hours than I had maybe the entire previous five years combined. How fitting that my friend who makes me laugh and smile to no end also makes me feel like we have miles to go still—miles more poems to write, essays to write, some of those *together*, more garden bounty (and woes!) to compare, more laughing and stomping our feet till we cry and almost get kicked out of a café again.

And miles and miles of watermelon smiles.

BLACK PEPPER

(A NOCTURNE)

 nocturne is a song of night, and black pepper is a heady summer night in your mouth, so let us sing of this darkness—

Never has the world seen so much rumble
and sail over such a small berry. Small,
dark meteor, perfect pop of fire—you docked
millions of boats to the southern coast of India,
kept so many folds of pale flesh awake and skittled
at night. Dreams of quicker trade routes, maps
and battle-plans inked in case anyone
tried to stop them from bringing back
sackfuls of peppercorn . . .

I dance and kick my way to the Malabar Coast of India—to Kerala, the land of my father and his ancestors, where the flowering pepper vine has been cultivated for millennia. The vine is a perennial ivy climber growing up to thirteen feet tall that adheres itself to a support tree or a man-made structure. It thrives in the Malabar region because of the heavy monsoon rains and elevation.

The dried-out drupe of this plant is known as a peppercorn, which can be black, green, white, or red. Black pepper is known as black gold, or the king of spices. Black peppercorns are made when the fruit is harvested right before ripeness, and they have the most flavor of all the types of peppercorns. The plant has simple, alternating leaves, which are oval in shape and produce clusters, or spikes, of fifty to one hundred fifty flowers. The small spherical fruits develop on the flower spike and start green and ripen to red-black. The drupes dry in the sun for several days, and the skin shrinks and darkens into a thick wrinkled layer around the peppercorn.

In ancient Rome, pepper was a status symbol, and the wealthy used pepper in desserts as a way to flaunt their fortune. So many mouths opened wide like caves for this spice, mouths accustomed to salt and sugar to flavor and spear their taste buds, and in those caves you will notice colonizers like book lice worrying the floor for bat waste until the whole ground vibrates. The popularity of black pepper may have been based on the desire by those of lower social status to imitate the elite.

The French sometimes paid their rent in peppercorns, a fragrant reckoning each month. One can imagine they did this under cover of night, for who wants to see you scrape spices together in a cloth sack and have it count as payment for a whole family to shelter and sleep and perhaps dream of even more fragrant futures?

In Bermuda, the annual Peppercorn Ceremony has taken place for more than two hundred years. During this event, Freemasons present the governor of Bermuda with one peppercorn on a cushioned silver platter in exchange for their rent of the Old State House. The idea of "peppercorn rent" is still practiced today in England and in other countries as well, where a nominal fee is charged to rent a property.

Once there was an Arabic myth of how black peppercorns came to be. Pepper was abundant in scary forests full of slither and shake. Pepper thrived in these forests, but it was difficult to harvest because the pepper trees were all guarded by poisonous snakes. In order to harvest it, farmers had to set fire to the trees and drive away the snakes. It was the fires that turned white peppercorns black and gave them their dry and shriveled appearance. After each burning, the trees would have to be replanted, which required money and time, and so that was why black peppercorns were so valuable.

Let us talk of more darkness—the dark gifts left inside tombs. Jars of peppercorns were found in Egyptian tombs, and slipped into the nostrils of Ramses II, who was mummified in 1213 BC. Cleopatra is said to have had lotions made with black pepper to rub into her skin. The fever in her arms and legs must have been like when you keep a goldfish in a dark bedroom, it eventually turns white.

In the Middle Ages, a pound of black pepper could free a serf, and many young maidens were married off with a black pepper dowry instead of gold or farm animals to plow a field. Even today, there is a Dutch phrase, "pepper expensive," which refers to a most dear and costly price.

For people who are plagued with sleeplessness or stress, taking a little bit of black pepper before bed is a relief. Try mixing some with powdered ginger in a tea, or with a teaspoon of honey. By increasing serotonin, which regulates mood, pepper is also believed to help anxiety disorders and depression.

Greeks and Romans loved to freckle their meat dishes with it, and leaders collected peppercorns in their treasuries, valued almost like gold bullion. No wonder Columbus and Vasco de Gama and all the rest of the early explorers risked it all, through the darkest of stormy seas on new moon nights with only the stars for guidance. Those months and months of night with no guarantee they'd even find land. Of course, I don't exactly feel sorry for them, those plunderers and murderers. Cooking with pepper (as with so many sugars and spices) is never neutral because of the weight of the peppercorn's history and *how* it traveled all over the world from where it was first grown.

I'm reminded of the nights I worked late, writing or revising on a deadline, and heard birds, a muffled chorus, but birds nonetheless. This would have been two or so in the morning, not yet sunrise, and so I thought it was most unusual. But when I asked one of my bird-watching pals about it later, he said I wasn't dreaming. What I heard in the middle of the night was the great migration taking place—birds leaving Central and South America and making good time to their nesting spots under the cover and safety of night. What must have these birds thought, hundreds of years ago, as they looked down and saw these baffling galleons bobbing in the night on the dark seas, in search of a small fire for their cavernous and hungry, hungry mouths.

MIRACLE FRUIT

Once upon a time I was considered ancient. Almost thirty and not married. *So old, too picky*, I heard aunties say in the kitchen. *Something must be wrong with her, the oldest grandchild and still not married. Always reading. Tsk-tsk.* But—I had a job. Tenure-track and I was good at it. Turns out, students love professors who are twenty-six and who genuinely care about them. I worked and worked, and saved and bought my own house. I could take care of my yard all by myself in scorching heat, wind, rain, and snow.

My father introduced me to miracle fruit a few years earlier, in the late nineties. He bought his first shrub from a roadside stand in rural Florida, and when he was excitedly explaining it on the phone, I have to admit I didn't quite believe him: *Okay, Dad! Sure, Dad! You eat this berry and anything you eat becomes sweet?* I was more dubious because he said he hadn't yet tried it, as the shrub hadn't even fruited, only had some flowers on it when he bought it. I just assumed he got tricked or something was lost in the translation from the man he purchased it from.

I talked to my parents pretty often, almost daily, and though they never said it, I think they were pretty worried about me all alone in my blue "dollhouse," they called it, with no plans to share it with anyone or anything. *How about a bird like Chico* (their cockatiel)? *A bird will notice when you are gone! You have to practice taking care of something, Aimee! Sige na!*

But I was in no hurry. I was taking care of *myself*. I dated plenty during my undergrad and graduate school years, and though I didn't have the words to explain it, it felt so good—if a little too quiet some days—to have a place of my own, a writing room of my own, and no need to trudge out into icy parking lots with my laundry basket. That was the dream!

So, months later, when a friend in New York City called to tell me of a miracle fruit party happening in a few weeks, I didn't even hesitate. With nothing to hold me down on weekends, I hopped a plane to see what this sweet fuss was all about. In the early 2000s, the miracle fruit berry started making headlines with its novel aftereffects. People were having "flavor tripping parties" in homes, restaurants, and rooftop hangouts.

The cardinal-red berry of the miracle fruit plant is about the size of a coffee bean. It's native to tropical West Africa. This unusual berry contains a protein called miraculin that was first isolated by Kenzo Kurihara, a Japanese scientist, in 1968. His report showed how miraculin alters the taste receptors in the tongue. After eating this berry, for about thirty minutes, everything you eat becomes sweet. A lemon is as sweet as an orange, a saltine cracker tastes like a cookie.

The miracle fruit party I went to was in the back room of a restaurant long since shuttered. I don't even remember the name of it, but the walls and maybe the lighting was red, the napkins were red, and there was a giant painting of a bull above the bar. There are suggested foods for "flavor tripping," but the ones we were served at the restaurant were: pickles, carrots, goat cheese, Guinness beer, rings of fresh red onion, limes, and salt and vinegar chips. The host from the restaurant instructed us to take a single fruit and chew it slowly, mashing it up and letting the berry juice coat your whole mouth for about a minute.

Then the fun began—all of us, about a dozen pals, began sampling each one of the "courses." Some noticed no changes at all with some of the foods, some had brighter reactions to most everything, but kept relatively calm. Some of us (I won't say who!) had wild, over-the-top reactions to every ingredient suddenly turning honeyed in their mouths. Until the Guinness—that was saved for last, and our host kept hyping it up through the meal. *It's dessert, you'll see, you'll see! Everyone says it tastes like a chocolate milkshake!* And even though our taste buds were clearly temporarily altered that evening, the beer was what we all cast our biggest doubts on.

We each were given another miracle fruit before we were served a pint of Guinness, perhaps to make sure the effect would be ever fresh, since the taste-bud switcheroo only lasts a half hour. After we were all served beer, we clinked glasses and cheered one another. I remember everyone's skin looked fuchsia, and we all seemed to be wearing clothes in shades of pink, but still gorgeous from the glow of red light bulbs in each sconce dotting the walls—all of us laughing, eyes sparkling like we are all getting away with consuming a most delicious nectar, such a sweet riot of joy. It felt illegal somehow. The host was right after all: if my eyes were closed, I'd have sworn the pint glass was filled with a creamy chocolate milkshake. I don't like to always admit it, but it turns out, my dad was right all along about this fruit—as he is about most things in my life.

And none of us at that flavor tripping party were partnered up. But we were *oohing* and *aahing* all night long, studying one another's faces, and O that was the time none of us had cell phones yet. I think a couple of us had a clunky something called a TracFone that required a refillable card for emergencies—we were just talking, talking, hooting, and guffawing nonstop, and though each dish brought out exclamations of incredulity (The goat cheese? More like a bite of *cheesecake!*) that party was *glorious*. Those few years of being single were glorious. All night we twisted our mouths into something ambrosial, delightful, tender.

I think we all knew it was fleeting as we wrapped our scarfs across our mouths—my friend Chris had just started hanging out with a guy who would soon be his husband, and I had a letter waiting for me at home from a cute writer named Dustin. My friends and I huddled on the corner trying to hail a taxi, and some of us shuffled up the street to catch the train—but that evening was one of those magical New York City nights full of friends and good food. Our taste buds were tingly, mostly back to normal by the time our last group got their taxi, but I couldn't help but feel that for that evening at least, everything was still sweet.

APPLES

Forget leaf blowers. The only buzz-saw-drone noise I can tolerate in fall is the whir of wasps slow-swirling drunk, knocking into one another in an apple orchard. When my boys were younger, apple picking meant a fun and early chance for them to have a "job," gathering fruit for our table and, later, perhaps a pie. They'd hoist a paper sack to their chests, insisting *Just one more, Mommy!* as they toddled around, clanging like wasps into each other down the orchard lanes, reaching their outstretched, chubby hands to pull one more Jonamac, one more Crispin, Cortland, or Snapdragon apple to toss into their bag.

My favorite is an Ida Red—white flesh, tinged with pink. This kind snaps clean in my mouth with a honey-cherry aftertaste on my tongue. A raw slice of it, or any apple, has such high pectin levels it can soothe a wound on tender parts of your body, like a cut on your lip.

There was once a time on this planet when all fruit other than berries were called apples. Tomatoes were *love apples*, dates were *finger apples*. Pomegranates were *grainy apples*. Bananas were just called *apples*. Scholars now believe the famous golden apples of Greek mythology were actually *oranges*. Unicorns were often painted with apples, supposedly their favorite fruit.

The first recorded instance of a father shooting an apple off his son's head was in the twelfth century. (This morphed into the Swiss legend of William Tell.) I remember hearing the tale as a kid and hating it. I didn't care that the dad made the shot and spared his son. All I could think about was the boy, how scared I was for him. I could imagine the tremble he must have felt standing there, waiting to be shot at by one of the grown-ups he was supposed to trust the most.

Decades later I picture the tremble of nineteen children, this time shot down in a school in Texas. And before that, the trembles in Buffalo at a grocery store, just an hour away from where I first became a mom, and where I took my sons to pick apples at our local orchard. And more recently, there's the tremble of kids shot while at an aquarium in Tennessee. There are not apples enough to cure this country's sickness. And it *is* a sickness. A wound on all our soft bellies.

Maybe if in the remembering of that terrible tremble of a child, in the rack and ruin of our own broken hearts as we scan the news of yet another mass shooting, perhaps one day we can finally vow to ourselves and to our children that what is more important than holding any weapons of war in your home is the promise of helping one another live another day. To look out for our neighbors (and their children) so that they might have the chance to clamor out of an apple orchard with quickened breath, a bagful of good fruit in each sticky hand.

GYRO

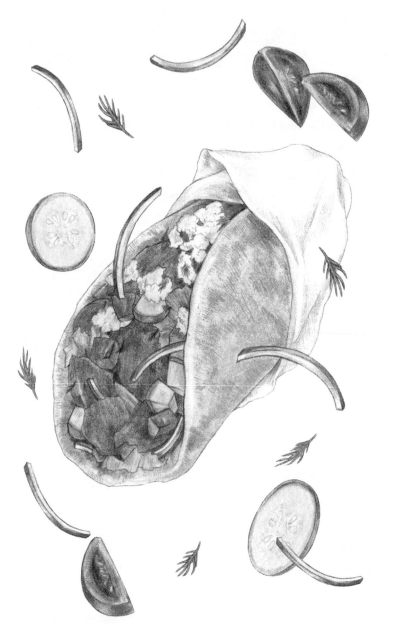

For over forty years, I've been chasing the most delicious sandwich I've ever had in my life: a gyro, pronounced YEE-ro, Greek for *turn*. The one I remember most vividly from my childhood was served by a now-defunct strip-mall restaurant run by the kindest Greek family. The only restaurant I've ever seen my father comfortable in. The waiters never made fun of his accent, or acted like they couldn't understand him. Nobody ever stared at us.

I've sent numerous emails, made half a dozen calls—all run into dead ends. In particular, I've been searching for a Greek restaurant that was housed in the 4341–4355 area of Sunburst Plaza that would have been in business at least from 1984 to 1986. All my leads for this strip mall in Glendale, Arizona, turn cold. It is as if I dreamed it up entirely.

Lamb gyros have been a Greek restaurant staple in the United States since the mid-1970s. Cones of gyro meat rotate on an estimated fifty thousand vertical broilers across the country, to be carved a few slices at a time and folded in pita bread along with a dollop of yogurt sauce. The meat is run through a four-ton grinder, where bread crumbs, water, oregano, and other seasonings are added. The pieces of meat, in the shape of an inverted cone, are placed on a tall rotisserie, which turns slowly in front of a source of heat or broiler. As the cone cooks, lower parts of the meat are basted with the juices. The outside of the meat is sliced vertically in thin, crisp shavings when finished.

We lived with just our father when we lived in the suburbs of Phoenix, as my mom was finishing up a contract at a mental hospital in Kansas at the time. I was plenty hurt, and missing her dearly, but didn't know how to say it, and I was perceptive enough even in fifth grade to know that if I cried, she'd cry, too, and *that* was the thing I could never abide. So I buried those feelings and, like a good daughter of immigrants, I threw myself into grades and school, a regular "Teacher's Pet" without really trying to be. Twice a month, Fridays meant payday for my dad as a respiratory therapist at the hospital, and that meant the rare treat of eating out, because my father loved to cook for us. My younger sis and I would beg for gyros, and I don't recall my dad ever saying no. Sometimes, he'd take us to the roller rink or to the Metro Center Mall (where the original *Bill and Ted's Excellent Adventure* was filmed), where he let us stop at a stationery store, and we'd each get to pick out a new sticker for our sticker books.

Getting take-out gyros was such a complete joy and respite from weeks spent without my mom. Sometimes we'd go night swimming and better yet, sometimes Dad would join us and point out constellations while my sister and I floated on our backs. I'd slowly turn and turn in the green-blue glow of the pool light like a starfish.

The closest I came to re-creating that gyro joy was in Greece itself. Most summers I teach poetry on the island of Thasos, and my husband and kids get to come along too. On that island, gyros are made of chicken or pork and stuffed with french fries right there inside the pita bread. The owners of a food truck on Alyki Beach that specialized in gyros knew our boys' names from their all-too-frequent visits while I taught poetry in the mornings. On weekends, we'd swim all afternoon, then grab a chicken gyro as we headed back to our seaside cottage. We've been doing this since my youngest was seven years old, so I hope my sons remember this "tourist sandwich," and I hope it reminds them of those long afternoons where they learned to swim in the Aegean Sea.

Just around the corner of the Hotel El Greco in downtown Thessaloniki is, for my money, hands down the best place for gyros in all of northern Greece. The gyro is so stuffed with crispy french fries, you can't even really put it down once you start eating, as you'll never be able to pick it up neatly again. It's about as big as a seven-year-old's head, and if all four members of your family order gyros, just barely able to fit it all on one small table on the café sidewalk, which almost empties out into the busy side street full of scooters zipping by.

Even though it is known as a sort of "fast food" these days, a gyro for me means a slowing down, taking stock of your family. It reminds me of the freedom I had as a kid in the eighties to walk to the little Greek restaurant in Arizona with a fistful of sweaty dollars. It reminds me, more recently, of weeks on a Greek island, seeing my boys dance traditional Greek zeibekiko in a cliffside taverna at night with a dozen or so strangers and my students, all of us dancing amid tossed napkins and broken dinner plates, as per tradition. It also reminds me of all those starry nights of floating in our pool as a little girl in the suburbs of Phoenix, the eldest child of immigrant parents, not fully knowing how to talk to them about things like *feelings*, but saying a silent prayer up to the stars for my mom to be safe, to watch over her while she worked in Kansas and away from us—and that she'd come back to us here in the desert—and soon.

PECAN

shuffled down to the hotel lobby in Florence, South Carolina, for some coffee, glasses on, hair piled in a messy bun on top of my head. The very first person I ran into exclaimed, "I can see you're about to GO NUTS!"

I'm known among my friends as never being able to have a poker face, and, it should be said, it's not really in my Capricorn nature to go, you know—*nuts*. So I imagine my frown and grimace was rather amusing (and obvious) to the man all dressed and ready to run the Run Like a Nut race later that day. *You can still register—there's still time,* he boomed. *No, thank you,* I said, *I just need coffee* . . . and somehow it only then dawned on me that all of this nuts lingo was connected to the South Carolina Pecan Music and Food Fest. It was, as I came to know later, the festival that *Travel + Leisure* named the "Best Fall Festival in South Carolina."

I was there in Florence for the Pee Dee Fiction & Poetry Festival, a literary festival filled with the kindest and most eager-beaver college students you could imagine, and I was forlorn to find out I'd be missing the evening's Pecan Festival headliner: Sister Sledge of "We Are Family" and other hits from the 1970s and '80s. But I still had a few hours to browse the booths filled with all manner of nuts and crafts, and even make a tiny stop at the pecan pub (just to look—it was not yet 10 a.m.!). I even took a pic with the giant inflatable pecan blown up and staked at the center of Main Street, all while nibbling on a pouch of my favorite kind that day: honey-crisp pecans.

The tree that was cause for all this celebration is monoecious, meaning the male and female flowers on a pecan tree grow separately at different locations on the same tree, unlike most other fruit. The female flowers bloom in clusters near the ends of the shoots in spring. The male catkins are born at the base of the shoot and along the length of the branches. Pecan flowers are pollinated by the wind. The very word *pecan* is from the Algonquin and means "nut requiring a stone to crack." Native Americans up and down the Mississippi River from Illinois to the shores of the Gulf of Mexico were eating them for hundreds of years before Europeans first stepped foot on the continent.

Pecan trees, armored with scaly, gray bark and waving their green leaves in the breeze, grow in neat, uniform rows upon the southern American landscape and yield more than 300 million pounds of thumb-size, plump, brown nuts every year. Native to the United States, they've become our most successful home-grown tree nut crop. My favorite pecans back home in Mississippi come from Moon Lake, an eleven-hundred-tree orchard in the Delta. The Callahan family fries their pecans and tosses them in a sweet and fiery sugar, selling them at our local community market. When I'm waiting for my boys to finish up their cross-country practice after school, I love popping over to this market, situated a block away from the school parking lot. I make a beeline to the Moon Lake pecan table.

There are over a thousand varieties of pecans, which come in a range of sizes, including mammoth, extra-large, large, medium, small, extra-small, and granular. Because I love seeing and reading about extremes in food, how charmed I was about the mammoth and extra-small pecans. When pecan trees are fully grown, they are about eighty feet tall on average, or about four giraffes high. It's a mighty and impressive tree. When pecan trees produce nuts so high out of reach, people throw heavy sticks upward to make them fall to the ground. What a nutty reign in this kingdom of branches and bird nests!

In South Carolina, one of the earliest growers of pecans was

John Horlbeck, an enslaver from Charleston. About ten years after he began to order his enslaved workers to plant pecan trees, his Boone Hall Plantation boasted fifteen thousand trees—the largest pecan grove in the world. You might recall Boone Hall was depicted in the movie *The Notebook*, as Allie's childhood summer home. But Boone Hall is actually where pecans came to be grown much quicker and more easily, thanks to an enslaved gardener known only as Antoine from Louisiana, enslaved at the Oak Alley Plantation, who successfully propagated pecans by grafting a superior wild pecan to "seedling" stock. This was the first time the nation had such a commercially viable grafted pecan tree—giving us nuts that previously were only considered a foraged food.

This new nut variety was such a hit that Antoine's newest enslaver, Hubert Bonzano, felt that these pecans were good enough to be exhibited at Philadelphia's Centennial Exposition in 1876, dubbing them "Centennial Trees" alongside displays that included no less than Alexander Graham Bell's telephone, the Remington typewriter, Heinz ketchup, and the right arm and torch of the Statue of Liberty. Each October, to harvest the nuts in Louisiana, enslaved people would hit these Centennial Trees with long poles until the nuts fell, then a second crew would come around and gather them on large cotton sheets. *Pecan South Magazine* notes that, in the 1904 Yearbook of the United States Department of Agriculture, this variety was described as:

> Size large, average; form long, compressed
> cylindrical, gradually tapering to the wedge-shaped
> apex; base conical; color bright grayish brown with
> rather scanty purplish splashes toward the apex;
> shell rather thick, partitions thin; cracking quality
> medium; kernel clear, reddish yellow, deeply and
> narrowly grooved, but quite smooth and separating

easily from the shell; plump, solid; of delicate
texture and flavor, quality very good.

Even though this deliciously buttery and glossy pecan grew in
popularity, it took the Centennial about fifteen long years before
any of these new trees produced pecans, and that, coupled with
the United States' rising demand for sugar and the pressure from
growers to plant the much-quicker-growing sugarcane, many of
Antoine's pecan trees were soon chopped down to make more
room for sugarcane instead.

The pecan is synonymous with the South because its natural
habitat is the nine southern states from Texas to the Carolinas on
the coast, given the high quality of the nut meat and the relative
ease of propagating improved varieties there. The pecan has become the "Queen of Nuts" in the United States, and other than
Mexico, the southern states are the only substantial producers
of pecans in the world. The pecan was the nut par excellence
for Native Americans. The word was also a signal of value, of
worthiness—a Miami Indian leader named Pacan signed treaties
at Fort Wayne.

During the self-described Pecan-palooza in Florence, I was
struck by how much music played a role. The games-of-chance
vendors had to really screech to be heard over the bands and
saxophone wails, and from the sample size of vendors and locals I spoke to, the correct way of pronouncing the word was
"PEE-can" not the dreaded "Puh-CAHN," though they said only
Yankees and Louisianans pronounce it that way. There was no
wind that day, but there was a popping. A crunch of shelled and
flavored nuts wrapped in wax cones for people to snack on as they
strolled. Spilled nuts on the street giving the numerous dogs on
leashes a veritable nut buffet as their owners walked on through
the booths, oblivious to what free snacks their dogs discovered

along the way. I had a plane to catch in a few hours, but I made sure to stroll around the booths to decide on what kind of pecans to bring home. I bought a couple of pecan pouches for my boys, as I try never to come home empty-handed, especially when a food festival is involved. A little souvenir to gather and tuck into my coat pocket, a treasure to share with them for the upcoming winter.

POTATO

My favorite part of my mother's chicken curry was the potatoes sopped in ginger, coriander, cumin. My father from Kerala was the one who taught her how to make it, but I confess all of us (my dad most of all) loved Mom's version best. The whole kitchen would emanate a peppery, earthy fragrance. When I'd come home from tennis practice and that smell greeted me, I could sleep the sleep I chase now as an adult more times than I'd like. She always simmered the potatoes just tender, not too spicy, but enough to give us a good light sweat when we ate. It was one of my favorite dishes to welcome me back when I visited from college.

I kept thinking I had plenty of time to learn it, and I took note of virtually every other dish she made, but somehow not her chicken curry. I try to make it at least once a season, but I can never get the sauce or the potato to feel just right. Not like hers. It's harder now for her to get around in the kitchen and my husband and I do most of the cooking when she visits. I scour cookbooks and try out the recipes, hoping to re-create even an approximation of her curry—to no avail. But I have faith I will one day conjure up those fragrant potatoes again for my family. If I keep trying new recipes and experiments, I'm bound to come close, right? One day?

For now—look up, look up: potatoes were the first ever food grown in outer space. The humble potato was chosen from all the food-bearing plants on our planet because of its excellent nutrition and ability to grow in extreme temperatures. In 1995, ten leaves from a potato plant were tucked into soil. Five cuttings were kept in a lab in Wisconsin, and five of them were packed into Space Shuttle Columbia and blasted into space. Just a few weeks later, marble-size potatoes formed from the plants in the lab, and hundreds of miles above Earth's surface, the space plants grew the same size potatoes, even in zero gravity.

Early Scots refused to eat potatoes because they were not mentioned in the Bible. Some even called the potato *devil apples*—claiming that potatoes caused leprosy, blindness, and too much lust. *"One potato, two potato, three potato, four!"* Misunderstood too: Captain Cook, Walter Raleigh, even Catherine the Great tried to convince people of the glorious crop but failed. Marie Antoinette and King Louis XVI finally convinced people to eat them by first wearing potato flowers in their hair and slipping blooms into their buttonholes. A royal adviser planted potato gardens all around the palace, with guards standing in bright uniforms during the day, purposely calling off the guards at night, effectively encouraging the locals to sneak out and dig up the potatoes and share with one another. Lord Byron lamented its aphrodisiac effects . . . *'Tis after all a sad result of passions and potatoes.*

The Quechua people of Peru have over one thousand words for this crop. They dance a two-step during harvest, pant legs rolled to knees—every one of their jumps pushes water from the bitter, marble-size tubers and into a *chuno* paste. In the black frost night, it dries and feeds a whole village for two seasons with a crystal starch.

Estar en las papas—to be in the potatoes—means a person has finally risen to afford more than a dry banana diet. In the Paucartambo Valley of Peru, one could read the soft earth like Braille, gather some on your own, each mound a possibility of sustenance. Tiny pineapples, coral snakes, purple gumdrops—anything but the brown oval spud shape I used to know. A small, flat one is called *mishipasinghan*, which means cat's nose; a knobby, difficult-to-peel kind is *lumchipamundana*, or *potato makes young bride weep.* The Acumbo village sees a surplus of the troublesome and bumpy kind in late summer. Housewives grind their teeth with each peel, stifle shivers into aprons, curse the abundant fruit.

Primatologists observed a female macaque monkey on Koshima Island in Japan soaking and washing a sweet potato in a stream before eating it. Soon, other young monkeys started imitating her, and then all the monkeys started preferring seawater to wash their potatoes, so they moved their colony closer to the shore to have easier access to the sea. Primatologists still don't know the exact reasons for this behavior, but they agree that the monkeys have developed a kind of culinary ritual with sweet potatoes. Ever since I learned about this, I probably think of monkeys washing their sweet potatoes at least a few times a month.

There is no constellation as of yet for the bodacious potato, a vegetable eaten by over one billion people a year. But maybe there should be—let's put one near the scales of Libra, waiting to measure the worth of how many people have seasoned and boiled and scalloped and baked and fried and hasselbacked and chipped and hashed and skinned and roasted and mashed the humble potato. One of my favorite things to do is treat my parents to any restaurant of their choice when we are together, be it in Las Vegas or Honolulu or Oxford. But no matter if the restaurants serve up their dishes on fine china or wax paper from a food truck, I have yet to find the comfort of those curried spicy potatoes of my childhood. Maybe the next time I will taste them will be on another planet, among glittered dust from another galaxy perhaps, another universe. But if you find the spicy curried potatoes before me, please keep them away from Ursa Major and Minor—the Big and Little Bear—bears *love* potatoes and have been known to scratch and dig and dig and dig to get to this vegetable most hearty and hale.

BING CHERRY

The truth about the first time I picked cherries in an orchard by myself is that I thought I'd be killed. All those times my parents told me to *be careful, be careful, always know your surroundings*, and I let my guard down, of all places, in a cherry orchard. It was the summer I moved to a tiny town in western New York, the first of my friends to land a tenure-track job, financially independent. For once in my adult life, I had no one to answer to. Which meant I was newly single—my grad school relationship had not worked out, and I simmered and stewed at that in a mostly white town with a population of 9,500. Which is how I found myself turning in to the hay-covered clearing of a cherry orchard just at the edge of our sleepy town. My car's license-plate holder at the time said "Elvis Presley's Graceland," and I'm guessing that's how the son of the owner of the cherry orchard found a way to drum up a conversation with me.

The son shuffled up behind me and offered a big white bucket and seemed so kind, so shy, with shaggy hair and fingerprints all over his thick glasses. Endearing almost. Looked to be in his late forties from the lines at the corners of his eyes. He pointed out which trees were "sweets," and which ladders led to "sours," best for pies and tarts and turnovers. Still others were Queen Anne cherries—the colorful, light pinky-peach-and-yellow globes all looking like they were kissed by a sunset over Lake Erie. He reminded me not to step on the top two rungs of the wooden ladders scattered throughout the orchard. He asked me if I was from around here, and when I said I just moved into town a few weeks earlier, he smiled and scuffed his boots back to his roadside stand.

I did make note that mine was the only car in the parking lot, and I did make note that the guy manning the cherry stand was a close talker—close enough that I could see his high gums and all the fingerprints on his thick eyeglasses—but there was so much fruit to be had, and he encouraged me to eat as many as I could while picking, because the next day a thunderstorm was rolling into town and that means the fruits would soon be split, opening their juicy innards up to the birds, bugs, and early rot.

I went right to the sweet darks, the Bing cherries, deep and red, full of body and seemingly full of blood. In the orchard, under the early July sun, I saw globes of fruit so bursting with light, it felt like an intoxicating fever dream, with trees heavy with dark red globes the size of shooter marbles. I couldn't believe the orchard worker said that I could sample as much as I wanted, because there was thousands of bunches of them—seven or eight to each cluster. I soon regretted my choice of canvas shoes, as the juice from fallen cherries soon stained the bottoms and sides of my shoes purple.

I climbed each ladder, and I've climbed ladders before, but this time it was different: when I reached into the trees I felt like a bird. I felt like no one could see me, and I had a whole unknown future just beginning to start in the academy. Each step made me a little light-headed, balanced so precariously into the air. I was on the cusp of a job I had wanted with my whole heart since I first started grad school; I'd assumed it would never happen, as professors were especially keen to warn us repeatedly each semester. *Have a plan B, C, and D—don't expect to ever land a job. If you do, great, but it's no given!* Here I was, just weeks away from starting a job teaching creative writing, and this balancing on one foot on a rung and reaching out with an outstretched hand toward such beautiful fruit over and over again made me feel both heady and anxious all at once.

The Bing cherry cultivar was developed in 1875 in Oregon, named after a Manchurian Chinese orchard foreman at the

Lewelling Orchards in Oregon, Ah Bing, who, according to various oral histories, stood over six feet tall. Bing worked at that orchard for thirty-five years and helped develop a new, plump variety, but after a visit back to China to spend time with his wife and children, Bing was never allowed back into the country because of the Chinese Exclusion Act, which passed in 1882. I think it is safe to say Bing never fully realized how much he impacted the cherry industry.

Farmers know to expect a Bing cherry tree to make as many as seventy-five pounds of fruit a year. These cherries are heart-shaped fruits with a meaty, purplish red flesh, and inside they contain a stone particularly good for spitting contests, because you can remove all the flesh pretty easily with your tongue and a few nibbles. The skin is almost black red, deep as wine, and the juice is, too, as my shoes could attest.

I remember the man told me to keep the stems on as much as possible when I plucked them—that makes them last longer in your fridge, he said. The drum of cherries tumbling into my bucket sounded like a sweet rain, a sweet thump in my heart, freshly picked from a breakup. My apartment was still not fully unpacked with all the stuff I brought with me from a poetry fellowship the year before in Madison. Here I was going to be a professor, I had cardboard boxes I used as coffee and end tables, and the semester was about to start in a couple of months. The apartment I rented didn't have a washer/dryer, so I had yet to figure out a laundromat situation in town. But here in the trees, I felt like I knew what I was doing, even though I had never been in a cherry orchard before.

As I was wandering to find another tree that hadn't been picked over, I felt the soft padding coming closer and closer in the straw-covered lawn behind me. When I turned around, there he was—the orchard keeper's son suddenly was standing really close to me, too close, really—and holding an old Elvis record in his hand. *When you're done out here I thought we could go inside and listen to Elvis records. Since you're a pretty big fan, huh?* I was so shaken from my cherries reverie I was scrambling, searching my brain how he ever guessed about my interest in Elvis, but then it dawned on me—he had seen my car's Elvis license-plate holders.

At this point we were way deep into the cherry orchard, so far from the highway, too far now for anybody who happened to pull up to the cherry stand to hear me scream. Now I was frightened. I took a step back, and he took a step toward me; I took another step back, and he stepped toward me. I found my words and said, *I think I'm done here. I'm going back to my car to get my purse so I can pay you.* And then I hustled back down the path that led to my car and the orchard stand. But he shuffled up to walk right next to me to say, *Oh, don't let me stop you if you're still picking—we can listen to records later, I'll be here all afternoon. No no, I need to get going, I need to make some phone calls*—my standard response for times like this.

As we tromped back to the orchard stand for what seemed like an excruciatingly long time, I picked up my pace so he could weigh my cherries and I could be on my way. As I was shaking the cherries into a kraft paper shopping bag, he asked me if he could take me out to coffee sometime later that week, or again listen to records, and when I didn't answer right away, he said, *Well, I guess you have a boyfriend, then! Yes, yes*, I said. *I need to go call him now.*

When I got into my car I breathed a sigh of relief. My hands were still shaking. I had ignored all the red flags and put myself in a scary situation, but I was entranced by the globes of fruit beckoning to me from the country road.

After I got home and moved things around in my refrigerator to accommodate the pounds and pounds of cherries I'd picked, I laughed a little to myself. What if I *was* interested? I'd have a whole orchard to pick whenever I wanted. Perhaps because I was still shaking from that creepy encounter, I wrote a poem flipping my feelings of fear, partly for fun, partly to excise any lingering uneasy feelings, and it was the first time I felt able to write since arriving at my new apartment:

The Woman Who Turned Down a Date with a Cherry Farmer

Of course I regret it. I mean there I was under umbrellas of fruit
so red they *had* to be borne of Summer, and no other season.
Flip-flops and fishhooks. Ice cubes made of lemonade and sprigs
of mint to slip in blue glasses of tea. I was dusty, my ponytail
all askew and the tips of my fingers ran, of course, *red*

from the fruitwounds of cherries I plunked into my bucket
and still—he must have seen some small bit of loveliness
in walking his orchard with me. He pointed out which trees
were sweetest, which ones bore double seeds—puffing out
the flesh and oh the surprise on your tongue with two tiny stones

(a twin spit), making a small gun of your mouth. Did I mention
my favorite color is red? His jeans were worn and twisty
around the tops of his boot; his hands thick but careful,
nimble enough to pull fruit from his trees without tearing
the thin skin; the cherry dust and fingerprints on his eyeglasses.

I just know when he stuffed his hands in his pockets, said
Okay. Couldn't hurt to try! and shuffled back to his roadside stand
to arrange his jelly jars and stacks of buckets, I had made
a terrible mistake. I just know my summer would've been
full of pies, tartlets, turnovers—so much jubilee.

In Wakefield Master's "The Shepherd's Play," the shepherds from the Christmas story were so poor and oblivious to the birth of Jesus that when they visited Mary and Joseph and the baby at the stables, they didn't have any formal gift prepared, but one of the men happened to have a cluster of cherries for the holy family.

Cherries also factor in a fifteenth-century ballad made popular by over twenty modern-day recordings—singers as varied as Joan Baez; Emmylou Harris; Peter, Paul and Mary; and even Sting all took turns recording a version. This ballad tells of Mary being so hungry on their trip to Bethlehem that on one of their breaks she asks Joseph if he could pick her some cherries alongside the road. Joseph must have felt extra petty that day, because he told Mary in so many words, why don't you ask whoever got you pregnant to get you some cherries. My favorite part of the ballad is that baby Jesus *from inside the womb* directed the cherry trees to lower their branches so that Mary could in fact reach them, and when Joseph saw this he freaked out and of course repented immediately:

There were cherries, there were berries,
As red as any blood.
Then Mary spoke to Joseph
So meek and so mild:
"Joseph, gather me some cherries,
For I am with child."

Then Joseph grew in anger,
In anger grew he,
"Let the father of thy baby
Gather cherries for thee!"

Then Jesus spoke a few words,
A few words spoke he:
"Let my mother have some cherries,
Bow low down, cherry tree."

The cherry tree bowed low down,
Bowed low down to the ground,
And Mary gathered cherries
While Joseph stood around.

Then Joseph took Mary
All on his right knee,
"My Lord, what have I done?
Have mercy on me."

~

Wood from the cherry tree is known to be particularly coveted to make into bagpipes, even though in Scotland it is considered bad luck to do so, as cherry trees are known as "witches' trees," and you are never to bring any young cherry branches inside your house, else face bad luck. But luck has followed me at the same pace as danger through a cherry orchard.

When I drove past that orchard the following spring, the white cherry blossoms had a delicate, earthy fragrance that reminded me of almond skin—a clean clip of breeze under my nostrils. That poem I wrote ended up being one of my most anthologized, most taught poems from my first book. More than twenty years later, I still get requests to read that poem during events and school visits. Cherry branches don't lower themselves to me to be picked, but it's all the better for me to rise up into the canopy, to sniff the heady air. Because below are the waste cherries, the ones that have fallen too early. I never stepped onto the top rungs of the ladder, either, but I loved to stay in that fruit canopy, that safe zone, even just a little while.

CONCORD GRAPE

For fifteen years I lived near the Grape Belt in western New York, which means each fall, it almost smells like someone is holding a cup of grape Kool-Aid under your nose—that's how fragrant and fine the roadways become that time of year. Both of my babies were born in the Grape Belt. This ribbon of land snakes through the southeastern shore of Lake Erie near the New York–Pennsylvania border for about fifty-five miles. When I was pregnant with each of my sons, we'd stop at roadside stands, where the dark-blue globes beckoned at us in the berry boxes made of pressed green cardboard. I ate so many during those early months, I joke my boys' brains and bones and hearts are made up of about half Concord grape, half french fries.

Other names for this grape are skunk grapes or fox grapes, because of that unique scent referred to as the "fox" note, which some have said smells like an old fur coat. Things that the grape farmers worry over: grape berry moths, grape leaf hopper, rootworms, and powdery mildew. I've always been charmed by grapes sweetening and swelling in the sun. But once, ten thousand fruits moved quietly in the dark, so intoxicating my friend who swerved us off the highway and into a grocery store in Indiana just because he needed grapes after a movie.

As with cinnamon, grape seeds have been found with mummies in Egyptian tombs that are at least three thousand years old. The Concord grape came to be from seeds dropped in a corner of Ephraim Wales Bull's garden by some local boys or a passing bird. That fruit ripened early and large and was particularly delicious. Bull shared the news of this aromatic fruit with neighbors like Thoreau, and his friend Nathaniel Hawthorne named the vine for the town in Massachusetts. Bull advertised the Concord as a native grape with a decidedly Yankee character—and it had "good shoulders," meaning, the broad clumps of grapes spreading outward at the top of a hanging bunch.

When the man who invented the Concord grape died, he was penniless. His epitaph read: *He sowed. Others reaped.* In the century following the introduction of Concord grapes, more of these purple grapes were sold than all other species combined. Today, growers harvest more than 336,000 tons in the United States. Washington State grows the largest number, followed by New York, Michigan, Pennsylvania, Ohio, and Missouri. The Concord variety, with their thicker skin, called a slipskin, makes up over 95 percent of the total grape acreage in western New York.

When I landed my first job as a tenure-track professor, I must admit that first year was extra lonesome. My whole family had recently moved to Florida—my parents to retire, and my sister to start a new nursing job. I was the only Nezhukumatathil north of the Mason-Dixon line. Most of my colleagues were my parents' age or married with young kids. I was a couple of years away from knowing any Asian American writers my age. But I wasn't totally alone. My friend Ron from my junior high school days lived in Dunkirk, the little lakeshore town next to mine, and since his house was within walking distance, we often met up for walks and scoops of ice cream at the Big Dipper. He kept me aware of all the local berry goings-on, the fruit and corn festivals; he knew the best You Pick stands within a forty-mile radius. We'd giggle over cute boys together and gossip about the mean girls from school who terrorized us when we were twelve. Ron couldn't attend the Silver Creek Grape Festival, and though I hated traveling alone those days, I did not want to miss it. So I gathered up my courage, slipped on some sandals, and headed out to Silver Creek.

The town's Festival of Grapes is the longest-running festival in New York State. In 2017, they celebrated fifty years of gathering in the name of the grape. My first and only vision of grape stomping was the same as that of millions of Americans: Ms. Lucille Ball in one old black-and-white episode of *I Love Lucy*. The Welch's Grape Stomping at the Grape Festival was the main event. The organizers rigged three tubs in a row, with a hole in the bottom of each that funneled the juice into a measuring cup. The contest would pit three people at a time against one another, and, watching a couple rounds, it was clear that the key to stomping the maximum amount of juice was of course to stomp as fast as you can, but to do so with a twist—as if you were a duck in a hurry and not able to make up your mind where to run, changing direction this way, then that. If you didn't want competition and wanted a quieter grape stomping with no peer pressure, the festival had a bigger plastic tub about the diameter of a kid's pool, where you could, for a small fee, stomp some grapes all by yourself for about a minute or so.

And so that's what I tried, since I didn't want to race anyone and just felt too shy in those crowds: too shy in case one of my students saw me all alone stomping away like I just stepped on an anthill, too shy to walk near the grape dessert tables because families plopped their folding chairs near them and it made me feel self-conscious that I was staring at desserts all by myself. There was a dessert contest to see who could concoct the best sweet treat made with grapes, but I left before I could see who won the contest. Even though I love live music, I was too shy to jam out to one of the cover bands, even too shy to buy a beer at the beer tent.

I saw the Grape Queen arguing with her boyfriend before the parade, her crown all askew. When she caught me watching them, she opened her mouth as if to say something to me, but her expression was serene. Inviting. I quickly dodged them and took my place alongside some septuagenarians on Main Street.

But what was I afraid of? I didn't have the words for it at the time, but it seemed like everyone I knew was married or settled in some way, and though my job and writing were all on the upswing, and I was awaiting the release of my debut book in the next year, my vision of what the future held with a family of my own was much blurrier. The possibility of having kids seemed like such an improbability, I dared not even share that hope with my best friends. Though I think my closest pals, like Ron, knew I wanted a family, they didn't say anything, as they knew my eyes would most probably fill with tears at even the mention of it. Here at the Festival of Grapes, almost every place I turned was filled with a reminder that I was alone. In hindsight, it was probably not the best place to hang out if you were freshly recovering from a breakup. And I was. And yet—

Something (besides the mouthwatering smells) pulled me back to the dessert booths. *I can do this*, I thought. I'd had to be the new girl so many times before, and there were no desserts back then to make it easier. But at the Grape Festival, the people who laughed the most and seemed to have the kindest faces hung out at the dessert tents, so I eventually made my way back there. I had my first taste of grape pie, and the kind woman who served it to me asked me my name and started to chat me up. I told her that pie was one of the best I'd ever tried, and from there she introduced me to her daughters, who, it turned out, lived in my town, twenty minutes away. And one of those daughters just happened to be the mama of the winner of the Grape Baby contest, and the lady who ran that contest was also introduced to me. I met the town librarian, and several ladies who knew some pals of mine at my church. The husbands eventually gathered around, and I could tell they were amazed that I'd driven there and found the festival by myself and even taken off my sandals and stomped some grapes for a bit in the community bin. Most women there didn't do anything by themselves when it came to festival-going.

I came to the Grape Festival looking to escape the double isolation I felt after my grad school relationship fell apart and being a junior faculty member of color in a predominantly white campus. And yet, I ended up meeting bunches and bunches of people who gathered me in as I was nibbling my slice of grape pie. Before I left, they demonstrated the best stomping techniques for future grape festivals and made sure I was sent home with a scoop of still-warm grape cobbler. What I remember most about these sweet people I just met is that they were all too happy to answer my questions—namely, how clean and safe was the wine if hundreds of people put their feet in it all day long? And though they were amused, some were outright laughing, incredulous at the questions, they all admitted they wondered about that, too, the very first time they stomped grapes. But they reassured me it was safe and clean, and not to worry, and it's true—according to *Wine Spectator* magazine, almost no human pathogens can survive in the high-alcohol wine environment, including *Staphylococcus aureus* and other bacteria that can be found on feet. For hundreds of years in some parts of Europe, "it was actually one of the few safe sources of hydration."

At the festival, I saw a number of hats and T-shirts that mentioned fun and goofy slogans about jelly like, "For the love of Jelly," "It's always jelly time," and my favorite, "Jelly donuts have fillings too!" But no one I asked could tell me how the famous Concord grape jam came to be other than it was "the Welch guy."

Turns out, in 1869, Dr. Thomas Welch, a minister and dentist, developed this early form of jam after trying to figure out how to keep grape juice from fermenting and turning into wine for his church's communion. His son Charles joined him in these experiments and introduced "Grapelade," which became a World War

I ration staple and was immensely popular with the soldiers who were clamoring for it again when they returned home.

It's been over twenty years since I first trampled grapes, but I can call up that sensation so clearly. And I'm not just talking about the sticky bursts of juice between your toes. I mean the sensation of walking into my home after being in the sun all day, surrounded by a bevy of new pals, and opening up my fridge to put in a sweet treat someone I'd just met had thought to share with me. And how the next day at breakfast, I didn't even warm up the cobbler, since it still felt like summer though it was already September, and the first silver maple leaves already started to slip off the branches. But dang, how juicy and cool those grapes popped in my mouth.

MAPLE SYRUP

Before I ever knew the name of the first full moon late in winter, I noticed it always glowed brightly. Perhaps we were just used to darkness enveloping the northern states. And maybe the faintest perfume of the woods in rural western New York smells just slightly different, the leaf and snow-crunch sweeter on the days of a slight melt. But that sugar moon, or sap moon, signals one more sampling of calm and quiet nights before the cacophony of frogs reminds us of the burst and blossom soon to come, even after the deepest winter.

I hope you'll forgive me if I don't miss much about the brutal winters of western New York, where I lived for fifteen years, tromping in knee-high snow as I walked to campus to teach, almost sliding off the Thruway too many times to count, and waiting out multiple weather-related strandings at the airport. But whenever February rolled around, just when we grew restless and a little weary from the lack of color all winter, from the scarves, boots, shovels, and Crock-Pot stews, we'd feel the flurries of my favorite type of snow, and I could almost anticipate the amber bounce and crumble of maple. A sugar snow is thick and heavy, and it hugs the base of the sugar bush (a forest of sugar maples made for tapping), while keeping the roots cool enough that they don't establish leaves just yet.

It takes forty to fifty gallons of sap to make just one gallon of syrup, with constant stirring and skimming off the foam, so I was all too happy to let the good folks at Maple Glen Sugar House do that magnificent work. I loved bringing my young boys up there just after a sugar snow to sample donuts and our favorite maple candies, small leaf-shaped sweets made of tightly packed maple sugar that crumbles and melts in your mouth. One year, the owners even let my four-year-old have the honor of tap-tap-tapping a spile into a tree in front of a crowded walking tour of the sugarhouse, and that's all Jasper could talk about for months, during bath time, during bedtime, and especially during our breakfasts.

If you can't get to a sugarhouse in late winter, the taste of maple candy may still be closer than you think. Pack some fresh snow in a casserole dish and leave it outside or in the freezer. Boil about a quarter cup of pure maple syrup until a candy thermometer reads 240 degrees F. Drizzle it right onto the snow in curlicues and dashes—and you've made maple candy. (But don't burn your tongue—it will be piping hot even on the snow!)

I've tasted several maple syrups from Vermont, like Summit Maple Farm's, and some from Belgium, spread on top of a *stroopwafel*, but I still find it quite difficult to describe the flavor. Thankfully there's a reason for my fumble: ninety-one unique flavors are actually at work, according to the Canadian Department of Agriculture. They drew up a "flavor wheel" to categorize the complex differences of maple syrup, organized among thirteen families: vanilla, milky, empyreumatic (burned), floral, fruity, spicy, foreign (as in fermentation), foreign (as in something added), herbaceous, plant (forest, humus, or cereals), plant (ligneous, as in firewood or sawdust), maple, and finally confectionery.

In sugaring season, fresh maple bacon and maple syrup poured over a plate of steaming waffles or a bowl of steel-cut oats signals the small promise of green bud and light slit into our kitchen just a little earlier each morning. We prepare for a sweet new season with actual sugar on our lips—like tasting a little bit of nectar as we prepare our garden, thumb through our seed and bulb catalogs, and watch the first shoots of crocus poke and push through the sugar snow.

CRAWFISH

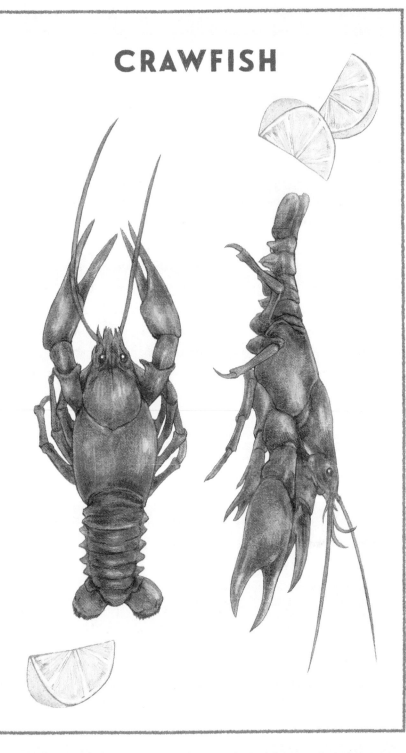

Suck the head, pinch the tail! My second year in the South, and I *still* couldn't get it quite right. The first time I ever saw a crawfish was when my fourth-grade science teacher in suburban Phoenix showed them to our class. Mr. Cass, my favorite teacher in all of elementary school, said he'd caught some, all I know is one day we showed up and there was a kiddie pool halfway filled with water and some rocks the size of my little fists right next to his desk. This beloved teacher was even the center of a poem I once wrote called "Mr. Cass and the Crustaceans":

. . . I have been trying to locate my fourth grade
science teacher for years. Mr. Cass, who

    gave us each a crawfish he found just past
the suburbs of Phoenix, before strip malls
licked every good desert with a cold blast
of Freon and glass. Mr. Cass who played

       soccer with us at recess, who let me check
on my wily, snappy crawfish in the plastic
blue pool before class started so I could place
my face to the surface of the water and see

    if it still skittered alive. I hate to admit
how much this meant to me, the only brown girl
in the classroom. How I wish I could tell Mr. Cass
how I've never stopped checking the waters—

       the ponds, the lakes, the sea.

Crawfish is what they are called here in Mississippi, but my husband grew up saying *crawdads* in Kansas. At all the *kräfts-kivor* gatherings in Sweden, they're called crayfish, and other names include craydids, mountain lobsters, yabbies, mudbugs, and crawdaddies. The biggest type of crawfish in the world is the Tasmanian, weighing about an average of eleven pounds—that's about as heavy as two two-liter bottles of soda. The smallest craw-fish is called a yabby, just a wee thing found in southeast Austra-lia's coastal lakes; around half an inch long, it weighs the same as about seven paper clips.

In the almost one-million-acre Atchafalaya Basin, North America's largest floodplain swamp, crawfish have thrived and lived among alligators, roseate spoonbills, and black-crowned night herons. Crawfish are quicker in water than on land, where they have a most unusual walk: they raise their front chelae up then down, and beat their paddle-like swimmerets, making it al-most seem like they are doing the butterfly stroke in a powerful reverse-whoosh through streams and swamps.

King Erik XIV of Sweden began the Scandinavian practice of *kräftskivor*—crawfish parties—when he farmed crayfish in the moat of Kalmar Castle. Three centuries later, the public adopted the Swedish king's crawfish-eating habit anew: crawfish perfectly intact, cold, and immersed in dill water, served up in boisterous gatherings outdoors. These alfresco parties became synonymous with Swedish culture, and today they are also a large part of Swe-den's culinary tourist draw in the summer. You can expect to find paper hats, streamers, and bibs in stores during *kräftskivor* sea-son in August and September each year, under the light of many moons—one of the memorable visuals of these celebrations is the bevy of paper lanterns strung up in backyards and restaurants featuring illustrations of a smiling full moon.

The Scandinavian *flodkräftor*, the crawfish endemic to the

Nordic area, were afflicted with a plague in the early 1900s that nearly left the species extinct, causing the government to take quick action; a law was passed that limited the fishing of crayfish to only a couple of months a year, with the season starting in August. In remembrance and as a reminder of this, the *kräftskivor* season begins then too.

In the South, crawfish boils typically take place March to May, because freshwater crawfish grow best in warmer temperatures and with lots of rain. Traditionally, the crawfish are stewed with corn, sausage, potatoes, and spices, then dumped on a long table so friends, family, and neighbors can enjoy a messy afternoon. And when I say messy, I mean roll-up-your-sleeves messy: use your hands to break the tail off from the rest of the body, peel the first ridge of the tail away, and then squeeze or suck the meat out. If you are feeling adventurous, open the body of the crawfish and suck the yellow stuff—an organ known as "crawfish butter" and considered the best part—out of the head.

The long table (six feet or longer, depending on how many guests you are expecting) is covered with newspaper or butcher paper. You can buy poker table–size ones with a hole in the center for a garbage pail underneath to place the freshly shucked tails and detritus during a boil. The simplicity of the boil is part of the appeal—you might have a large wastebasket nearby for all the shells and legs, and a roll or two of paper towels for your slippery (and spicy!) hands.

Here in the American South, it's considered almost chic to have a clandestine crawfish connection—you can casually disclose that you know a guy, or have a neighbor who knows a crawfish farmer and can get you a good deal.

It's boil season as I write this here in Mississippi, as evidenced by the crawfish carts and trucks setting up shop in every gas station in town, often coinciding with the season of Lent. Having a

crawfish boil is a fairly new culinary party—eating these crustaceans was associated with poverty until the late 1950s, when a
crawfish festival in Breaux Bridge, Louisiana ("the Crawfish Capital of the World"), helped rehabilitate that mostly white percep-
tion of economic status. In the decades that followed, crayfishing
was a sociable activity for all of society—during the week there'd
be outings to catch them, and by the weekend they'd be thrown
on a table, blazing red after a boil.

Crawfish can be kept as pets, too—my teacher used to tell
me they'll eat just about anything, including their molting debris for its high concentration of calcium. I remember seeing one
nibble on what looked like a ghostly cartoon drawing of a crawfish and then realizing it was eating its own shell-crackle. And
mostly, even though I've loved participating in boils here in the
years since I moved to the South, it becomes harder to participate. People can't seem to agree on whether or not crawfish can
feel pain when boiled alive, but the thing I can't get over is that
most crawfish taste bitter from the stress hormone cortisol being
released during boiling. Just knowing that has stopped me from
eating them, which has given cause for many a southern pal to
look at me a little askance.

I remember begging my dad in fourth grade to take me to
school earlier than the school bus so I could have time to check
on my pet crawfish, feed her bits of lettuce, and change out her
water before the first bell rang. I loved watching her stare back
at my bespectacled ten-year-old face from under the rocks I arranged for her in the kiddie pool. My sons are just now, after
seven years, beginning to have that slow southern drawl when
they ask for crawfish or when they say boil, which now sounds
closer to how they'd normally say *ball*.

It can't be helped, can it? The South crawls into us like a skit-
tery crawfish. Even the word *crawfish* puckers the mouth when

you say it. All the variations of what is known as the *southern accent* may just be my favorite kind of accent in the world (other than Filipino accents), and when I hear my sons say things slower, drawn out just a bit more than they did seven years ago, their accents sound like the pause before a party, something like a celebration of a southern spring in their mouths.

BUTTER

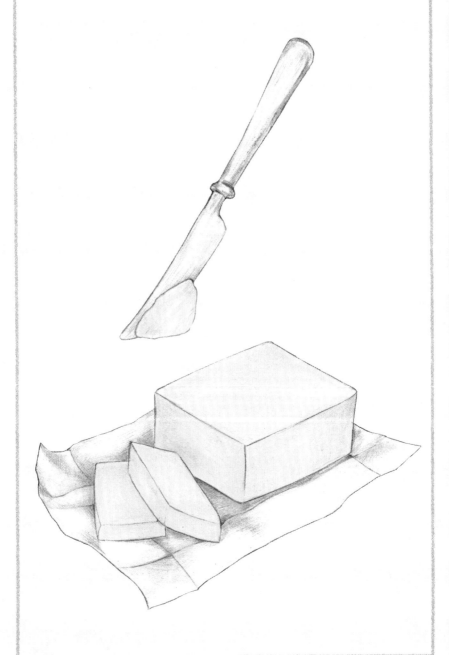

n her poem "Butter," Elizabeth Alexander writes, "we are . . . glowing from the inside / out, one hundred megawatts of butter." Butter (and all its variations) makes me, and many of the people I love, happy. I want to get to the bottom of this—the buttery bottom of the pan if you will—for answers.

~

Sumerian clay tablets from 2500 BC, for instance, describe a well-established cult whose followers brought regular offerings of butter to their temple in order to satisfy the dairy desires of the goddess Inanna. Sumerian writings also reveal a reverence for the act of butter making, in passages like, *The rocking of the churn will sing for you, Inanna . . . thus making you joyous.*

~

According to *TasteAtlas* online, the ten most popular butters on the planet are:

10. Mantequilla de l'Alt Urgell y la Cerdanya (Spain)
9. Beurre d'Ardenne (Belgium)
8. Beurre Rose—Marque Nationale du Grand-Duché de Luxembourg (Luxembourg)
7. Beurre de Bresse (France)
6. Trabzon Butter (Turkey)

5. Mantequilla de Soria (Spain)

4. Beurre d'Isigny (France)

3. Niter kibbeh (Ethiopia)

2. Beurre Charentes-Poitou (France)

and the most popular butter in the world, probably due to the billions of people in my father's home country of India alone:

1. Ghee

For over three thousand years, Hindus have placed metal cups of ultra-rich and luscious ghee at shrines for Lord Krishna. Ghee is perfect for tropical regions, as it is shelf-stable. Once you add this flavorful butter to a dish, it automatically becomes a jamboree in your mouth.

~

The oldest known butter-making technique still in use today is remarkably similar to current methods, minus the goat: Farmers in Syria skin a goat, tie the dried skin into a leak-proof vessel, fill it with milk, and hang it from a tree, swinging it back and forth until bits and chunks of butter begin to form.

~

Butter was precious to ancient Norsemen, and many were buried with barrels of butter to carry with them into the afterlife. Their fondness for butter was so widespread that Europeans referred to Viking warriors as "the butter eaters."

~

Back in the fifteenth century, the Catholic Church banned its followers from eating butter during the forty days of Lent. However, Catholics could pay a fee to the church if they wanted to free themselves from the butter ban entirely. So many French Catholics opted to give money rather than forgo butter that the revenue generated from Lent butter fees became a substantial funding source for France's Rouen Cathedral. Today, Rouen Cathedral is colloquially known as the Butter Tower.

~

A crock of butter, symbolic of fertility and wealth, was a customary gift for newlyweds in England up until the 1500s.

~

As an adult it still feels extravagant to get "buttered" popcorn at a movie theater, but I only recently found out it's not butter at all, but oil with flavorings and coloring on it. But no one wants to say yes to the question, "Would you like oiled popcorn with that drink?"

~

Around the Easter holiday, the grocery stores and Polish markets in western New York sell butter lambs for your table. The ones already boxed up have a small snip of red ribbon where the neck is supposed to be, and peppercorns or cloves for the eyes. But let's be honest—most of these lambs look more like a butter cloud. At the fancier markets in Buffalo, you'll see lambs under glass cases piped from a pastry bag onto a piece of tagboard covered in wax paper.

This beloved Easter tradition has been a part of Buffalo's culture for nearly one hundred fifty years, and the butter lamb's origins can be traced back to the Polish immigrants who settled in Buffalo in the late 1800s. In Poland, the butter lamb is known as *Baranek wielkanocny*. When Polish immigrants came to Buffalo, they brought this tradition with them, and it quickly became a staple in the local community each Easter season.

~

I resisted the butter lamb for years, until both boys were old enough to participate in their first Easter egg hunt together. The boys must have been two and five, or three and six—and of course they were delighted and astonished about the Easter Bunny, whom they had talked about and worried about for weeks. Worried because there were impending snowstorms, and how could a bunny make it through to our house, and carrying eggs to boot?! But as Dustin and I started getting the table set for Easter dinner, one of them noticed the butter lamb on a small blue plate, and it was over.

Suddenly they wanted butter, and prior to that day, I believe they had never wanted butter (or even known what it was) in their lives.

One wanted the lamb's red ribbon scarf.

The other cried as Dustin absent-mindedly scraped off

part of the lamb's head to butter a roll—

My oldest claimed dibs on the eye, so suddenly amid the ham, the deviled eggs, and the asparagus spears, we had two toddlers pouting over a peppercorn.

I looked across the table at my husband, his eyes shining, both of us trying not to laugh at our predicament.

The deformed butter lamb shone brighter under the lights above the dining table. It started to melt and pool on the dish.

Perhaps it was more fraught than I remember, but today I only remember that dinner with gladness.

We must have been somehow, some way—in fact, I *know* we were—glowing.

RISOTTO

At the base of the Lightning Research Center in the Swiss Alps, you can forgive me if I thought everything a little more *charged*. And when you have two kids under ten and you and your husband have, together, never left them since they've been born—every quiet dinner seems electric, a rare magnificence. So when I say a little hotel in Switzerland produced the most marvelous mushroom risotto of my life, please forgive me the delirious swoon-sizzle, because until that point I thought I hated risotto.

Turns out, I'd just had a series of unfortunate risottos. What changed my mind? How did a bowl of this creamy, traditional northern Italian rice dish come to jolt and haunt me and hold the standard for all risotto dishes I've chased down and tried (and failed) to re-create?

Risotto is, at its core, rice cooked in broth and a bright oil. You don't need a large pantry for a basic introductory risotto—it is fairly easy to gather ingredients. Traditionally, onions, butter, broth added to short-grain rice, topped off by a grated cheese, most likely Parmesan, cooked and stirred carefully until it swirls creamy.

Legend has it that in 1574, the apprentice to Valerio of Flanders, a master glassmaker in Milan, loved saffron so much, he used it in his artwork, even using it in his tints of stained glass. His friends and family used a pinch of saffron in his risotto as a joke, but it turned out so delicious that it eventually became a local sensation and is now known as *risotto alla Milanese*.

When my boys were six and nine, Dustin and I had soured on our academic jobs, the small town and campus becoming an increasingly untenable place for a mixed-race family to live and feel like *thriving*. In such a toxic and creepily racist department, emotionally we were just barely surviving and keeping smiles on our faces for the sake of not scaring the boys. At night, I'd cry to Dustin that I felt like I couldn't breathe in that tiny town anymore.

But that fall brought a dazzling invitation to be a guest of the Grisham estate, John and Renee Grisham's seventy-acre sprawling former property that they had donated to the University of Mississippi on the outskirts of Oxford. The weather was bright and clear and warm for outdoor play. In short, we could breathe and make art again. We remembered what it was to grow with such artistic and smart community members, who welcomed us with open arms.

Soon, I was asked to guest teach and read poetry to the boarding school of my dreams—TASIS, the American School in Switzerland. Dustin and I didn't think we'd be able to travel as we had no family or sitters set up yet, but my in-laws once again offered to come down to Mississippi to help out. We knew in our hearts that the boys would relish being outside all day long with their grandparents, but my mind raced with dread and I double-checked on our wills to make sure everything was updated to recognize our youngest too. It's morbid, I know, but the boys only knew what it was like to be with at least one of us whenever there was work travel involved.

Especially for Dustin, who was on sabbatical and taking on the lion's share of the childcare and the school pickups, this was a trip not taken lightly. But we had come to that age where so many people we knew were having marriage troubles. Perhaps that was in the back of my mind, perhaps to steel it a little bit to give me strength to go overseas with my husband and to leave the kids behind. And why not? Dustin is a partner in every sense of the word, a present father who doesn't tune out or throw his hands up in the air when our boys ask questions for about forty-five minutes straight. He knows their preferred breakfast fruit, what size socks each of them needs, how much stovetop popcorn my youngest likes to have in a bowl for a snack, and can tell just by looking at them if they told the truth about brushing their teeth or not. Dustin also knows when I haven't written that week, and the perfect amount of grapefruit juice and vodka I like, and exactly what my favorite mug is in a messy and crowded cabinet of coffee cups. He knows the dentist and doctor appointments for the whole family and keeps track without being told. And truth be told—he does this all when he's *not* on sabbatical and teaching full-time at the university. You don't get to have that specific knowledge about your beloveds unless you take note of details, unless you are there for your family, unless you ignore prescribed gender caretaking roles. He just steps up.

And so, on one of my free days in Lugano, we decided on a day of sightseeing and riding the funicular up the Monte San Salvatore and seeing the literally breathtaking views in the western Alps almost three thousand feet above sea level. At the amethyst peak of the mountain is the Lightning Research Center inside the San Salvatore Museum, where you can bolt a bright coin of knowledge into your neck like bolts in the pale green monster's neck of the early *Frankenstein* movies, back when no blood was ever seen, never pulsed or throbbed on-screen. And when we made the long journey back down the mountain on the red funicular, all I could think was *What happens if the cables snap and we slide down this striped Swiss mountain made of oceanic quartz on its edelweiss-covered face and crash?*

Spoiler: We did not crash, and I was so elated. We might have been a little too dizzy with glee but soon we were lost after shopping for chocolate souvenirs for our boys, parents, and my students.

We wandered around with no phones, our faces and fingers thoroughly rosy by the time the streets felt familiar, and we knew we were close. We climbed up the familiar cobblestone street of our hotel, hungry and chilled. So when the waiter at our hotel said we have a special risotto, I surprised myself by saying yes.

There were tablecloths, cloth napkins—those two things alone felt so indulgent to people who are used to asking kids to clean off the dining table of Lego creations and Matchbox cars each night. Our kids play back home with their grandparents and what have we done? First, we dared eat the finest risotto, drink wine over a white tablecloth. Maybe we'd be struck by lightning yet. But there was no lightning, there was only this piping-hot bowl of mushroom risotto placed before me, each bite creamier than the last. The mushrooms themselves were just a touch salty, the buttery, short-grained rice seasoned like it had been cooked in a stew of chicken and sweet carrots.

The three types of rice for a risotto are arborio, vialone nano, and carnaroli. The ultrastarchy arborio is the one you'll most likely find in grocery stores in the United States, but all three are high in amylopectin, a starch that dissolves in the cooking process, giving risotto its characteristic creaminess and slightly sticky texture.

When it's time to do the final *mantecare*—the final stirring of the risotto—you'll add a golf-ball-size scoop of butter and let it ooze and melt. Where risotto usually fails is in this last spot, either not stirring enough or letting it sit too long on the stove. Risotto is a dish that must be served *immediately*, no waiting for guests to leisurely finish their wine or take a quick call first— and maybe that's why this mushroom risotto in particular tasted extraordinary. Maybe it was the dizzying whirl around a town we weren't familiar with and temperatures dropping quickly. I couldn't even let myself dare to dream we'd make it back in time for a warm meal, but after somehow not eating for hours, that was my fervent hope.

When we finished our wide bowls of risotto, we held hands across the table. We might have held hands more in those four days in Switzerland than we had the last four months—and well, it was a good reminder of how we'd even ended up there in the first place. We were a team. We had each other's backs. Hand in hand. Otherwise, we wouldn't have been able to dine together on a random Wednesday overlooking Lake Lugano, which was just starting to sparkle from house lights along the water's edge.

We didn't yet know that we'd soon be selling our home to make a move to Mississippi, a move to the Deep South, new books for both of us brewing, and a new campus—all in the span of a year. We didn't yet know we were about to make the decision to raise our boys in that beautiful green land, but we could feel something good changing, crystallizing in the air. Even in thinned air I still reached for his hand. Before our fingers laced, I'm certain the waiters gathering around the hostess stand at the end of the evening noticed it, and I'm sure the old ladies who stared at us on the funicular earlier that day saw it, too: the spark, the crackle, the brilliant strikes of light between us.

COCONUT

n 2013, people in the Maldives thought there was a husky, potentially cursed suspect accused of tampering with a presidential election. Police were called to confiscate a young *coconut* left near a polling station at the Guraidhoo Island School because locals worried the fruit was bad luck or even carried a spell in its flesh to influence the election.

~

If someone calls a brown person a "coconut," they mean "white on the inside yet brown on the outside." A person who likes to experience Western (white) culture despite their Desi upbringing. Other variations on names for Asians include being called a banana, an Oreo, and I'm sure there are other delicious alternatives. I myself have never been called one of these things to my face, but I definitely have heard the term whispered about others for liking the "wrong" type of music, wearing the "wrong" type of clothes, or even living in the "wrong" (read: all-white) neighborhood.

~

Ninety-nine percent of coconuts used for oil in Thailand have been harvested by monkeys. Pigtailed macaques are used to harvest coconuts so much that there are actually training programs for these monkeys, and competitions are held each year to find the fastest coconut harvester monkey.

~

You can mail a coconut. If you clearly label it, the U.S. Postal Service will ship it. I remember my ex-boyfriend had a pal in Hawaii who kept sending him coconuts from Molokai all the way to his apartment in Washington, D.C. No message was ever written on them. But maybe that was the point, because she knew I'd see the coconuts piled in the corner of his room.

~

About six hundred people a year die from coconuts falling on their heads from great heights.

~

Pink coconut water is the result of oxidization of the sugars in the coconut. Temperature, age, sugar content, and how long the water has been exposed to air can all affect the coloration of coconut water. It's like the way an apple turns brown after being cut. Just as you can eat a brown apple, you can safely consume pink coconut water.

~

A male monkey can collect sixteen hundred coconuts per day, a female about six hundred, while the average human can collect about seventy. But there is a kind and peaceful place in Thailand, founded on the basis of Buddhist teachings, called the Somjai Saekow Monkey Training College, where monkeys are humanely taught how to pick coconuts with no violence or force or shouting. The working monkeys get massages and are even checked for red ants during breaks. The monkey trainers at the school say they understand the worry and fuss from animal rights activists, but their monkeys are taken good care of and treated like pets. In fact, they say working conditions are comparable and many times even better than those of working sheepdogs, oxen, or dogs sniffing for drugs in airports.

~

Coconuts can travel up to about one hundred days in the ocean and still germinate when they hit shore. The three holes in a coconut resemble a little monkey face, but they are actually germination spots for a new tree shoot. Just off the coast of Australia some octopuses use coconut shells for their shelter.

~

On my first visit to India to meet my grandparents, my Aunty Mabel must have seen me tired and slumped over from jet lag, because one day she swooped me up into her cinnamon sweet-smelling sari and shooed me into the courtyard. She had collected a whole stack of coconut shells from the property, and she handed me one for each hand. *We will be horses today, Aimee! You watch!* She clomped and clomped them in a slow motion; it sounded like a bona fide canter, then a full-on gallop so loud that my dad came running out to see why there was a team of horses in the front yard.

~

One of the problems with throwing out the word *coconut* as a hurtful jibe toward those who don't conform to reductive cultural stereotypes—besides the fact that it is just flat-out insulting to say one's actions betray their upbringing, lived experience, and culture—is that it assumes there is one correct way to be Asian. But there is room for *all* to canter or gallop ahead in my herd. My people are people who won't ever judge the smoothness of your fetlock or the color of your feather.

WAFFLES

The day after my husband's thirty-ninth birthday, I wake and see the cold windows already steamed up, and for a brief moment, I think all the killings were just a nightmare.

The shootings took place in an elementary school the previous day. and instead of going out to celebrate Dustin's birthday as planned, we canceled the sitter and stayed home with our boys, Pascal then in first grade, and Jasper still toddling around in footie pajamas. Even at that age, the boys could discern any flicker of sadness in our faces, and when they couldn't understand why we weren't laughing more for their daddy's birthday, it broke my heart to explain to them that some kids were hurt that morning at a different school. No, scratch that—at that age, they would have asked a bajillion questions. I would not have said anything. Would not have wanted to tell them how kids Pascal's own age had their bellies blown up by a senseless crime. Would not have wanted to face their questions. Would not have wanted their giant brown eyes to grow wider if I told them someone shot so many kids. Somebody's babies. Now that I think on it, I am sure of it. I know we gently told them about school shootings eventually. But not that weekend. Not that week, either, and soon it would be my birthday, then Christmas. We told them, but not just yet. Let them have one more holiday without that knowledge. They were seven and four, for crying out loud.

The steam from the waffle iron fogs up my glasses when I peer over the strong shoulders of Dustin. We decide on making it a Waffle Morning. We didn't call it Waffle Morning that day after the heartbreaking school tragedy, and that wasn't the first time we made waffles together as a family. But that was the first with *intention*.

Let's be honest: my husband is the one who makes the waffles. He gets up early with the kids when I have late-night writing sessions, though we try to go to bed at the same time when possible. The kids know it's better for all involved if *he* makes breakfast, and better when I make dinners. Then I'm not bleary-eyed, sliding a spatula in the garbage disposal for example. And Dustin isn't forgetting the onions he was sautéing that have now turned into a pungent crisp, making our nonstick pans stick.

The obelio is a version of waffle that can be traced to ancient Greece, consisting of a cereal-based batter cooked between two metal plates. Later in medieval France and Germany, wafels had a honeycomb pattern, and still others had intricate star and flower shapes indented into the batter as it cooked. By the eighteenth century, *waffle-frolics* were a popular type of jamboree. Even Thomas Jefferson brought a long-handled waffle iron from France when he sailed home to Virginia, and by then, waffle-frolics were not just a fad in the new colonies, but a full-on regular occurrence.

Our family's Waffle Mornings consist of a simple gathering. Some sliced fruit for toppings, someone brings sausages or bacon from a local farm, and on the table is a small bowl of confectioner's sugar to sift over the waffles like the prettiest snowfall, if one would like (my boys would always like). Sometimes family friends or neighbors come over, but we keep them much smaller than a full-out waffle-frolic, which normally has dozens of people gathering in a "luxurious feast with the crowning dish, waffles," the main event of these lively jamborees. Though we have Waffle Mornings year-round, I especially love them in winter, when I wake to boys still in their flannel pajamas and our chunky Chihuahua who used to pace under the waffle iron in case any batter drippings should fall his way. My favorite winter weekends: fireplace on, and coffee already waiting with little clouds of steam rising from my favorite peacock mug, our little dog curled into a croissant at my feet.

Our boys are teens now. After I come home from giving readings or talks, I don't have to make any requests. Dustin makes it so: Waffle Mornings still happen at least once a month. Sometimes more often—the more chaotic our life, the more waffles. The more fellowship with our loved ones. When our boys were younger, what took place after a Waffle Morning in the summer might be: bubbles, water table, scrawling hopscotch blocks and Lego characters in the driveway, sandwiches on the back porch, naps, and popsicle hour (about four o'clock in the afternoon).

Now, after a Waffle Morning in the Mississippi heat with teens, it might be: skimming the pool, helping me weed the garden beds, then all of us jumping into the sun-bright pool till lunch, when our sunscreen runs its course, sandwiches on the back porch, naps, and popsicle hour (still about four o'clock). And I cherish that we still have this time together, and Dustin and I work hard to make the boys *want* and ask for this time with us too.

Every time we send the boys out the door to school, we take a chance. Our boys endure school shooting drills, and we have no solid answers for their questions about Why and What-ifs. So we try to make their return to our home feel safe and comforting. Not to be oblivious of their worries, but to slow down and come together around a table of fruit-topped waffles with our beloveds who are with us. To take nothing—no thing—for granted, even the squabbles, the wet towels left on the floor. To be able to wake up and have the scent of coffee and waffles baking in the air. Our partners and kids with rumpled hair.

Growing up, I never saw mixed-race families in books or movies depicted happily sitting around a table, let alone Asian Americans, who come together in the mornings with joy (okay, maybe a touch of grumpiness once in a while), excited about what an open Saturday might hold for them—together. What does that do to a person who never sees anyone who looks like them joyfully gathering for a meal in any books, television, or movies? You begin to wonder if it is possible, if it is something you dare hope for in the future. But Dustin and I are determined to make this not just a possibility for our kids, but the norm. Even if they still don't see it represented nearly enough in media, even now. And I am acutely aware that using the word *frolic*, or the word *jamboree*, in an essay that starts so dark, doesn't seem to fit. But I always want to fight for the light, for the warmth of a family that my sons can count on, no matter the chaos and fear created in the world. When I think of those sweet faces, the teachers' faces, the principal, all gone now from this planet, but forever young in my mind—it catches my breath, I scuff my slippers in the dark, little lightning strikes. These are the sparks. These are the sparks.

HALO-HALO

The double-double of the word on your lips when you say halo-halo promises you will never be in a bad mood when you order it from a restaurant. Normally, my mom and I are usually together for Mother's Day, but in 2021, she opted to stay put. My boys and I head to Memphis instead—home of her favorite singer, whose motto, *Taking Care of Business*, she learned soon after she arrived in this country. Elvis Presley's wrought-iron gates, custom inlaid with guitars and musical notes, mean to signal: superstar. I don't even remember a time when his music did not play in our house. My parents have pictures of me on tip-toe in my footie pajamas, trying to reach the inside of our stereo console to play his records. One of my parents' first dates was an Elvis Presley concert in Chicago. In other words, he was a pretty big deal for my family.

We've learned Elvis's favorite food from his mama was nothing fancy—bananas, bread, and peanut butter, even when he became a millionaire. So of course I brake on Macon Road when I spy a picture of halo-halo, my mom's favorite dessert, and drag my whole family inside for some ice-cold joy first concocted on the other side of the planet.

Maybe because in Tagalog *halo-halo* means mix-mix, I carry a special fondness for it. After all, my mom married a man from India who also loved Elvis, even shaped his sideburns like his and had a thick black pompadour like him, so I am *mix-mix* too. And because I married the sweetest white man from Kansas, our boys are also *mix-mix, mix-mix!*

With halo-halo, you never know what you are going to discover and when. Each spoonful promises a richness of delights: shaved ice, nata de coco, diced jackfruit, sweet beans, sweet corn. The signature pop of purple from a scoop of ube ice cream shouts *Yes*, and if you're lucky, they'll put leche flan on top.

Go ahead, mix it all up: mix-mix.

Almost twenty years later, when I type this on a summer day that tops over a hundred degrees here in Mississippi, a movie about Elvis Presley's life is topping the box office charts, and Oscar buzz floats for its lead actor. I can hear our boys yelp and giggle and splash with their pals in the backyard. The boys are listening to the *Elvis* movie soundtrack blasting on a speaker outside. Black, brown, and white teenage boys make our pool *mix-mix* now too. Our sons never had a chance to play with so many different kinds of families when we lived in western New York.

Once, when we visited a frozen Niagara Falls in the middle of an ice storm, a man told me he wanted to be with me forever after knowing me for just weeks. *How are you so sure,* I asked him, *how do you know so soon?* And the man, who is now—you guessed correct—my husband, simply said, *I just do.* Snow continued to fall and collect on our eyelashes—it was that cold. The edge-splashes of the Falls were already frozen and starting to bloom into white mushroom-mounds of pure ice. I looked up into his green eyes and saw Dustin was steady, serious. He didn't waver or try to blow it off, like what he said might have been an accident. He remained. I had no idea what our cups would hold, what our future would be. But I *knew* then, surrounded by so much ice—it would be sweet.

A CODA: LECHE FLAN

Means crème caramel made of milk. Means special occasion. Means Mom and Dad are in a good mood, so don't mess this up. Means we're probably having company. Means you'll probably have to comb your hair and wear a dress. Means you'll probably be asked to dance your "Billie Jean" dance routine in front of the whole party. Or to play the flute before leche flan is served in small triangle slices to everyone, even though you can't ever quite get a grip on reading music correctly. Means no horsing around or throwing a ball in the kitchen when Mom is balancing the llanera mold ready for the smooth and even bake, without airholes or cracks in the gooey, caramelized surface, because if you or your sister bump her when she's carefully sliding this into the hot oven, you'll be smacked with one of her slippers, her tsinelas—I warned you—*Thwap!*

Leche flan is traditionally prepared by steaming, although baking in a water bath is also common. The gentle and slow cooking process helps the custard set properly without curdling, keeping it fluffy and light. Leche flan requires sugar melted on a stovetop to create caramel, which lines the bottom of the mold, before pouring the custard mixture on top. The creamy, silky custard creates a wonderful contrast with the caramel sauce's dark, piquant flavor. After cooking and cooling, the leche flan is usually inverted onto a serving plate, allowing the caramel sauce to slide over the soft and silky disc of custard.

The Spanish colonization of the Philippines brought about the building of many churches in the sixteenth century. One of these churches, Saint James the Great Parish Church, is in the town square of Bolinao, the municipality where my mother grew up in Pangasinan. These churches used black coral stones and egg whites, millions of them, as an ingredient in the durable argamasa mortar the buildings were made from, which helped to bind and protect the building materials from wind and typhoon.

Resourceful cooks saw all the egg yolks being tossed away into the river, so instead of wasting them, they concocted a whole bevy of desserts, the leche flan among them. There are hundreds of variations online and in cookbooks, but the one I fell in love with first is my mother's recipe, just five ingredients: about a dozen eggs, sugar, vanilla, and milks—condensed and evaporated.

But I must admit that I've never been able to re-create her exact recipe just so. No cracks, no holes from air bubbles popped. And that makes me wonder what, if anything, my own boys will remember about being home during various celebrations. Have I created a singular dish that can hold the place of leche flan as a signifier for celebrations and jamborees for over five decades? What, if anything, do I make that is a classic dish in their mind? Don't get me wrong—I can make a pretty solid apple dumpling, any type of cobbler, crumble, cake, or crisp. I can make homemade fruit-filled hand pies, most cookies, and for my boys' birthdays, I had always made their cake from scratch—once I baked a dinosaur cake complete with a chocolate-covered Rice Krispie volcano erupting in the middle of it with homemade strawberry-jam lava. Another year, it was a six-layered rainbow piñata cake where Skittles spilled out of the center when you sliced it.

Will my boys remember the class treats of beach cups—complete with paper umbrellas, crumbled graham cracker sand, and gummy sharks tucked inside cerulean Jell-O? Will they remember the cupcakes with homemade whipped frosting, or the hot chocolate spoons for their kindergarten classes that held a tiny bear-shaped cookie under a blanket of chocolate and sprinkles, so it looked like the bear was tucked in ready to sleep in the scoop of a teaspoon? Nope. We already *know* the answer is no, and they haven't even finished high school yet.

But they also won't remember the time you spilled a whole new bottle of peppercorns, and the glass shattered everywhere and pieces even landed in your dog's fur. The time it was International Day at their school and they were the only ones who didn't bring a food to share because both you and your husband forgot. What I do hope they remember is a warmth in our house. One you can't re-create exactly even if you tried. It just happens—the smells of their daddy barbecuing, even during a tornado watch, the noise and pop of our fireplace, the textures of towels and blankets fresh out of the dryer, the colorful dishes and mugs set at the table. I don't even remember the times my mom didn't use the right number of eggs or had big cracks striping into the surface of the leche flan, but if you were to ask *her*, she would remember when and on what occasions those mistakes happened. All I know of her leche flan is that, to this day, it is the best—the creamiest, lightest flan I've *ever* tasted.

Funny how we beat ourselves up trying to get a perfect recipe, a perfect dessert, a perfect party in the books. There's so much that goes into making a meal that might be forgotten in mere weeks. Not everyone will remember the place settings, the sprig of coral and lavender zinnias. The plump raspberry garnish in their drink. But that's not the point when it comes to loved ones. You heat up the waffle iron. You shave the ice. You rescue the egg yolks. You have to. You make something new with what you have. You take the extra bit of time. It doesn't always turn out how you think it should.

You make it anyway.

ACKNOWLEDGMENTS

There is no magic wand or formula to get a book like this into your hands without a cadre of big hearts and big eyes. My biggest thanks to the following for shepherding this into the world.

Some of these essays appear (some in different incarnations) in the following magazines. Thank you to the editors of *Orion*, *Gravy*, *Sierra*, and *Prairie Schooner*.

Some poems are snipped from my own books:

- "The Woman Who Turned Down a Date with a Cherry Farmer," *Miracle Fruit* (Tupelo Press, 2003).
- "The Origin of the Mango," *At the Drive-In Volcano* (Tupelo Press, 2003).
- "Mr. Cass and the Crustaceans," "The Pepper Kingdom," *Oceanic* (Copper Canyon Press, 2018).

Hugs and gratitude to my elegant and effusive agent, Laura Blake Peterson at Curtis Brown, who dealt with more anxious and giddy calls than anyone not related to me should have to bear—all this through a pandemic and loss of loved ones—but through it all was my steady guide, my lighthouse through this world of books. To Fumi Mini Nakamura—I'm so honored to get to work with you again. Your illustrations are magical and marvelous, making me hungry at all hours of the day, ha! To Jenny Xu for your enthusiasm and to my editors Gabriella Doob and Sarah

Murphy for their questions and insights every step of the way. To Holly Frederick at Curtis Brown. To Team Ecco, especially Helen Atsma, Meghan Deans, and Cordelia Calvert. To Jennifer Chung for her artistry.

Blue Flower Arts, especially Anya, Miyako, and Rebecca, for keeping me connected to my readers; what a joy to meet them and teach all over the planet. Thank you for watching over my travels and sharing my books and teachings.

Joseph O. Legaspi—what a dazzling world this would be if everyone had a friend like you, with razor-sharp wit, compassion beyond the horizon, and sartorial flair to boot! Ross Gay—bright star, plating up potatoes and possibilities, always. Sarah Gambito is always guaranteed to make me laugh or cry, and I wouldn't have it any other way. Oliver de la Paz, Jon Pineda, Patrick Rosal, Beth Nguyen, Adrian Matejka, Matt de la Peña, Jane Wong, Sharon Wong, Mark Steinwachs, Sara Sutherland, Ron Degenfelder, Margaret Renkl, the Manganaros, the Monroe family, the Bruce family, Robin Hemley, Leah Umansky, and Lisa Kwong.

Erin Austen Abbott; Wright Thompson; the Atkins family; the Fennelly/Franklin family; Jarred Wilson; Deb Whitman; the entire team at the independent bookstore of my dreams, Square Books in Oxford, Mississippi; the (mighty) Milkweed Editions team, especially Yanna Demkiewicz, Judy Braus, and the North American Association of Environmental Educators (NAAEE); Jason Mark and the team at *Sierra* magazine for all of your support and cheers; the mighty editorial eyes of Sumanth Prabhaker and the whole *Orion* magazine team, for giving me a column in which many of these essays first bloomed.

The Parsons family—so much of the travel in this book could not have happened without you being such kind and generous grandparents. Thank you to the DeRosa family and my nephew Dominic for his enthusiasm; the David Citino family; Russell

Motter and the Iolani School in Honolulu; and Christopher and Allison Wilkins Bakken and my co-faculty from the Writing Workshops in Greece Program.

Dr. Christopher Love and his sweet family, Julie Frazier-Smith, and the American School in Switzerland for hosting me (again!) with the most exquisite hospitality and mountain air. Kim Rogers and Carol Wilcox for giving me the treasure of place and time in Hanalei Bay, Kauai, to work on these essays. What richness of spirit and hearts you offered up to me! Thank you for introducing me to so many beautiful writers during that dreamy week. Ranger Karen at Yosemite NPS; Ian Cheney and Meredith DeSalazar for icebergs and reindeer; Scott Pollack and the staff of the Minnesota Marine Museum—thank you for your vision and dreaming BIG. The Nevada Humanities Council, the Indiana Humanities Council, the Mississippi Humanities Council, the Southern Foodways Alliance, and the Mississippi Book Festival. Dr. Jo Angela Edwins of Francis Marion University and the Pee Dee Fiction and Poetry Festival for giving me time to "go nuts" with pecans.

Dr. Cynthia R. Greenlee, sharpest of eyes and fabulously extraordinary editor—coming through with such care and sheer intelligence. Thank you times a gabillion for encouraging me to dig and ask hard questions of myself and the world. Thank you for believing in this book, and for seeing me.

Chef Vishwesh Bhatt, for making me feel like a rock star, always greeting me and my family at Snackbar in Oxford, but it is *us* who are the lucky ones who get to partake of your scrumptious menus with South Asian nods—one of the first things to make me feel like we could make a home in Mississippi.

John T. Edge was one of the first people I met in Mississippi. He offered up books when I was lost, and when I was stuck, he knew exactly how to help, due to his encyclopedic knowledge of food histories. Thank you for just being "good people."

Dr. Joshua Nguyen, brilliant and most dependable of research assistants extraordinaire—thank you for gathering up the sugar and kernels; Simms Powell, chef in training and talented fruit forager, and the entire Parikh family of Jackson, Mississippi— thank you for taking me in again and again.

My coworkers and students—thank you for your grace and cheers and willingness to try new things. Working alongside y'all is a true honor. My champion of a chair, Dr. Caroline Wigginton, and the Office of the Provost and College of Liberal Arts at the University of Mississippi—thank you for your support.

Haiku, our dearly missed wily Chihuahua—he was small in stature but big in personality, semi-famous for his magnificent side-eye—my constant companion for a decade, my "heartbeat at my feet" (as Edith Wharton said) as I wrote my last two books, but passed away while I was finishing edits on this one.

My parents, who showed me love indeed and in deed, *and* by the offering up of bushels and bushels of fruit. You modeled being curious about the stars, what is in the oceans, and our garden. I somehow never remember a time growing up where we didn't have a delicious dinner together. You did this all while working such long hours in hospitals, and I'll never be able to repay that bounty, though I try every day.

Jasper and Pascal—I hope you look back at our travels these years with a delicious fondness because it's really *you two* who showed me the world. Thank you for knowing and understanding when I needed quiet and when I needed jamboree. You're the sweetest treasures of my life, my double delight. Watching you grow into spectacular humans has been the greatest wonder— you two are the best poems I will ever write.

Dustin—over twenty years by my side, again and again I give thanks for you. I have never laughed harder than I do when I'm with you. It takes a special (and patient!) partner in every sense of the word to live (and make a nest) with a poet. All the school lunches and drop-offs for our boys, the driving around for sports, airport pickups—all while you teach, coach our son's baseball team, and be a writer yourself—I mean . . . no part of this happens without *you* as the anchor of our family. Thank you for taking care of my art and heart. I'm so grateful my journey is linked with you—step by step, bite by bite.

FURTHER READINGS AND RESOURCES

Albright, Mary Beth. *Eat & Flourish: How Food Supports Emotional Well-Being.*

Bakken, Christopher. *Honey, Olives, Octopus: Adventures at the Greek Table.*

Balingit, Abi. *Mayomu: Filipino American Desserts Remixed.*

Banerji, Chitrita. *Eating India: An Odyssey into the Food and Culture of the Land of Spices.*

Bass, A. L. Tommie. John K. Crellin, ed. *Plain Southern Eating: From the Reminiscences of A. L. Tommie Bass, Herbalist.*

Bhatt, Vishwesh. *I Am From Here: Stories and Recipes from a Southern Chef.*

Bittman, Mark. *The Best American Food Writing 2023.*

Cailan, Alvin, with Alexandrea Cuerdo. *Amboy: Recipes from the Filipino-American Dream.*

Courage, Keith, and Marcelle Bienvenu. *Pecans: From Soup to Nuts.*

Dimayuga, Angela, and Ligaya Mishan. *Filipinx: Heritage Recipes from the Diaspora.*

Edge, John T. *The Potlikker Papers: A Food History of the Modern South.*

El-Waylly, Sohla. *The Best American Food Writing 2022.*

Farrimond, Stuart. *The Science of Spice: Understand Flavor Connections and Revolutionize Your Cooking.*

Fisher, M. F. K. *The Art of Eating.*

———. *How to Cook a Wolf.*

Flandrin, Jean-Louis, and Massimo Montanari, eds. *Food: A Culinary History.*

Ford, Eleanor. *The Nutmeg Trail: Recipes and Stories Along the Ancient Spice Routes.*

Gay, Ross. *The Book of (More) Delights.*

Gilbert, Sandra M., and Roger J. Porter, eds. *Eating Words: A Norton Anthology of Food Writing.*

Goldman, Amy. *Melons for the Passionate Grower.*

Gollner, Adam Leith. *The Fruit Hunters: A Story of Nature, Adventure, Commerce and Obsession.*

Hobart, Hi'ilei Julia Kawehipuaakahaopulani. *Cooling the Tropics: Ice, Indigeneity, and Hawaiian Refreshment.*

Irwin, Sam. *Louisiana Crawfish: A Succulent History of the Cajun Crustacean.*

Jaffrey, Madhur. *Climbing the Mango Trees: A Memoir of a Childhood in India.*

Ko, Lauren. *Pieometry: Modern Tart Art and Pie Design for the Eye and the Palate.*

Lebo, Kate. *The Book of Difficult Fruit.*

Lin, Grace. *Chinese Menu: The History, Myths, and Legends Behind Your Favorite Foods.*

Lopez-Alt, J. Kenji. *The Best American Food Writing 2020.*

Lundy, Ronni. *Sorghum's Savor.*

Mamet, Zosia, ed. *My First Popsicle: An Anthology of Food and Feelings.*

McWilliams, James. *The Pecan: A History of America's Native Nut.*

Mintz, Sidney W. *Sweetness and Power: The Place of Sugar in Modern History.*

Naglich, Mandy. *How to Taste: A Guide to Discovering Flavor and Savoring Life.*

Norman, Jill, ed. *The Story of Food: An Illustrated History of Everything We Eat.*

Nostrat, Samin. *Salt Fat Acid Heat: Mastering the Elements of Good Cooking.*

Nye, Naomi Shihab. *The Tiny Journalist: Poems.*

Ponseca, Nicole, and Miguel Trinidad. *I Am a Filipino and This Is How We Cook.*

Ray, Janisse. *The Seed Underground: A Growing Revolution to Save Food.*

Rubin, Gretchen. *Life in Five Senses: How Exploring the Senses Got Me Out of My Head and into the World.*

Sharma, Nik. *The Flavor Equation: The Science of Great Cooking Explained.*

The Bitter Southerner, eds. *Food Stories: Writing that Stirs the Pot.*

Taylor, Joe Gray. *Eating, Drinking, and Visiting in the South: An Informal History.*

Vaughan, Mehana Blaich. *Kaiaulu: Gathering Tides.*

Walter, Eugene. *Hints and Pinches: A Concise Compendium of Aromatics, Chutneys, Herbs, Relishes, Spices, and Other Such Concerns.*

Wong, Cecily, and Dylan Thuras. *Gastro Obscura: A Food Adventurer's Guide.*

Young, Kevin. *The Hungry Ear: Poems of Food & Drink.*

FOOD WRITING PROMPTS

When food or drink is mentioned in writing, the mind races and rushes for associations and/or remembrances. Food or drink often has a subtext—a layering or, forgive me, a *flavor*—tinged with grief, joy, shame, desire, nostalgia. No matter your experience level, here are some writing possibilities to try:

1. What is the earliest memory you have of trying a new (to you, at the time) fruit? Describe where and when this happened and try to explain the texture and smell as precisely as possible.

2. Taste the rainbow: write a poem or lyric essay in seven segments, with each segment of the piece representing a food a color of the rainbow: red, orange, yellow, green, blue, indigo, violet.

3. Spice is nice: What is your favorite spice? Coriander? Cardamom? Cumin? Look up the healing properties and/or folklore of that spice and create a scene where a character uses that spice to heal someone.

4. Write a poem in one sentence about a meal you had with someone who is no longer on the planet or with whom you don't have a relationship anymore.

5. Describe what your perfect last meal would be on this earth. Make it as many courses as you like, right down to beverages and dessert.

6. What food would your character serve someone they had a crush on? Someone they wanted to impress? Someone they despised or who hurt their feelings? Be as precise as possible.

7. Write about your favorite guilty pleasure food.

8. Make an abecedarian essay (twenty-six sentences or paragraphs, each one starting with the letter of the alphabet) about your relationship to cooking (or takeout!).

9. Try growing your own food or herb—something you've never grown before—and take notes! Use a pot and a well-lit window if you don't have access to a garden plot. Write two to three journal entries a week tracking the progress of what you grow. If it doesn't work out, try another herb! Tomatoes and strawberries work great in pots! Basil and parsley grow easily for herbs!

10. Make a poetry comic with at least six panels about a mistake you made once while preparing food. Use a blank sheet of printer paper for each panel.

11. What food or drink sends you immediately back to childhood, no matter where you are? Write *why* it captures your childhood, and see if there are any connections to your present day. Let us smell, feel, taste, hear, and see what it is like to eat/drink this too.

12. Write about the most exquisite dessert you have ever tasted.